To

Dan

From all at

Superquinn Finglas
3,11,73

Best of Luck
In the future

Jim Fitzpatrick

Alan Fairbrother

Veronica Wood

Paul Reilly

Jim O'Hara

"Feargal Quinn has written about the essence of his incredible success as one of the world's greatest retailers. It is based on a simple principle — he cares. He cares about everyone associated with his operations and above all he cares about each customer.

"Many say the customer is king or queen but seldom mean it. For Feargal it is the truth. Walking through a Superquinn store with him is like walking through his home. He knows everyone and everyone knows him.

"His secrets are all in this book. We should be grateful Feargal has shared them with us."

Donald R. Keough
President and Chief Operations Officer
The Coca-Cola Company (USA)

CROWNING
THE
CUSTOMER

How to become customer-driven

Feargal Quinn

Raphel Publishing
Atlantic City, New Jersey

CROWNING THE CUSTOMER

Copyright © 1992 by Feargal Quinn

Cover Design by: Donna Huyett/Studio 151

Manufactured in the United States of America

ISBN 0-9624808-2-7

Distributed by **Acropolis Books, Ltd.**
13950 Park Center Rd., Herndon, Virginia 22071
Phone: 1-800-451-7771

Éist le fuaim na h-abhann mar
gheobhaidh tú iasc

Listen to the sound of the river
and you will catch fish

(Old Irish Proverb)

CONTENTS

INTRODUCTION
By
Dr. Anthony J.F. O'Reilly
Chairman, President and CEO
H.J. Heinz Company

FEARGAL QUINN belongs to a band of Irish people who grew up during the 1950s, in a world busy remaking itself after the depression and wars that had dominated the previous generation. Many of us had an unlimited belief in our ability to make an impression on that new world, a boundless (and largely unwarranted) confidence in our capacity to achieve anything we set out to do.

Thirty years or so later on, Feargal Quinn is one of the world's most respected innovators in the fiercely competitive world of retailing fast-moving consumer goods. He is a much sought-after speaker on the international lecture circuit, and he is a director of the United States Food Marketing Institute and of the Paris-based C.I.E.S..

What is perhaps remarkable is that he has achieved this standing without moving from his original Irish base. He runs a modest supermarket business that rates somewhere around #291 in the world ranking of supermarket chains by size. However, you begin to get an idea of his achievement when you learn that his Superquinn company ranks #20 in the world in terms of sales per square foot of selling space.

That Quinn must know *something* is evidenced by the number of visiting businessmen that beat a path

to his door by the sea on the outskirts of Dublin—
supermarketers from all over Europe and the U.S. as
well as top management from the giant firms like my
own who market their products through the
supermarket channel.

What they discover is what readers of this book can
now find out for themselves, and its application
extends way beyond the world of retailing. His
message is that there is indeed a magic way to success
in business. It is based on old-fashioned ideas that
have always been around but have been more and
more difficult to apply as modern life has thrown
complications in our way. At our mother's knee we
all learn that "the customer is king," but not so many
work out just how to apply such a high-flown
concept in real life.

Feargal Quinn opened his first store in 1960, a small
premises of less than 5,000 square feet and with a
total staff of eight. Today, he employs more than
2,000 people and has a sales area of over 300,000
square feet. From the beginning his approach was
driven by a search for excellence, a single-minded
determination that his company would be the best at
whatever it decided to do. Another part of Feargal
Quinn's retailing philosophy that soon emerged was
his emphasis on customer service, founded on a
determination to build an organization that would
always try to see things from the customer's point of
view.

This dedication is delivered with a quirky
consistency. To remind his store managers that their
real job is on the selling floor, he always instructs his

10

architect to give them small, dingy offices. People who work at Superquinn's headquarters have sometimes found their desks have disappeared while they have been on vacation, as a gentle encouragement to get out more into the stores. Feargal Quinn himself likes to hold meetings when walking around the floors of his stores, a preference that can surprise people used to more conventional business encounters.

As he demonstrates in this book, he is committed to the notion that business should be fun — but his approach is deeply serious in intent. Top of his priority list is the need to stay close to the customer, and he feels that this is a lesson everyone in business can usefully learn. He believes that customers of any business want a high level of personal service, of the kind that can be provided only by human beings rather than machines. He has proved that investment in people pays off in terms of increased business which pays for the additional staffing costs.

It is perhaps this aspect of Superquinn that has attracted most attention around the world — the fact that a high-service operation can be provided without charging higher prices for it. In other markets, the received wisdom has been that a high level of service is something the customer has to pay for in higher prices, but in Ireland this has always been impossible because the grocery trade is so competitive.

Many times in business we hear the cry "back to basics!" Feargal Quinn is someone who has made that journey, and this book chronicles the path.

CHAPTER 1

*How a small (5 ft. 4 in.) Irish grocer
came to write this book*

WHAT CAN THE OWNER of an Irish supermarket
chain teach American readers about customer
service?

That is a question I would have thought a very
strange one back in 1961, when I made my first visit
to the U.S. I went to Dayton, Ohio, to attend a course
in "Modern Merchandising Methods" by the great
Bernardo Trujillo.

I went to kneel at Bernardo's feet for the same
reason as so many other foreigners did, people who
have since become retailing leaders in many countries
around the world: because we all regarded the U.S.
as the cradle of retailing expertise, the marketplace
that could teach us all we needed to know.

As my own business grew and prospered in Ireland,
I kept going back to America like a horse going to its
watering hole. Several times a year I would take a
plane from Dublin and cross the Atlantic in search of
new ideas, new ways of serving the customer better.

And I became so convinced of the value of these
visits that I started a practice that continues today,
whereby all our store managers and promising junior
managerial staff also come to America to learn.

Later on, when I was asked by the Irish Government
to become chairman of the Irish postal service, I had
to learn about another kind of "retailing." Again I

turned to the U.S. and to the U.S. Postal Service in particular, for know-how about the latest direct marketing techniques.

So when I sat down to write a book about what I had learned in thirty years of serving the customer, it was certainly not with an American audience in mind. There was nothing I could offer to the people who had taught me all I know. Or so I thought at the time.

I actually wrote the book in the first place for my own staff. When my company Superquinn was smaller, I not only interviewed every applicant for a job but made sure that I spent a great deal of time with each new member of our team during their first few weeks.

In this way it was easy to see that each new person learned very quickly what were the things I believed to be important, and where the priorities were in our small company.

But as the company grew, I found that among the duties I had to delegate to others was that of training. And in doing so I had to find a way of explaining to our trainers what was the thinking behind the way we had been running our business since the first shop opened in 1960.

When I finally got around to putting my thoughts to paper, many people suggested to me that the lessons of what I had written applied just as much outside the company — not just in retailing, but also in any other kind of business activity. And that is how what I investigated as a staff manual came to be published as a book in Europe.

14

As soon as it appeared over there, the same thing happened again. Many of my friends in U.S. business who were kind enough to read the book said to me that they thought it would be very useful to people working in American business.

At first I was skeptical: to me America was not only the home of modern retailing techniques, it was also the birthplace of all the best management books!

What could I offer, that hadn't already been said before? Would it not be like teaching my grandmother to suck eggs, as we say in Ireland?

True, my business friends said, there is nothing new in your book. It is very basic, very elementary. But that is the whole point. You deal with the simple things about customer service that we in America sometimes forget about. Our approach to business has become so complicated that we find it very hard to make the basics *happen*, in our dealings with customers.

"We know all the theory, what we can learn from you is how to put it into effect."

This rang a bell with me, because it mirrored my experience on the other side of the Atlantic. Over there, as in American, everyone these days is "customer-driven." Or at least, everyone pays lip-service to the customer-service ideal.

That was one of the big changes of the 1980s, spurred on by the publication of such books as *In Search of Excellence*.

Across the face of world business, putting the customer first suddenly became respectable again — after several decades during which the whole thrust of business development had been technology-driven (in the case of manufacturing) or systems-driven (in the case of services).

But believing in the customer-driven approach is one thing: delivering it is quite another.

If we judge from what we see around us, how many people and many organizations deliver?

And yet a dramatic change is exactly what you would expect, given that everybody is now preaching customer service.

That's because the customer approach *should* turn upside-down the way a company does everything. By customer-driven I mean a company where *all* the key decisions are based on an overriding wish to serve the customer better. A company where everyone in it sees serving the customer as the *only* business that they are in.

That's the principle by which I started my supermarket business in 1960. I did not do so because I believed in it as a theory. I did it because it came naturally to me, and also because my first business experience as a teenager convinced me of it.

Once the company was up and running, I found two things out very quickly. Firstly, that the customer-driven approach pays off.

For us in Superquinn, it gave us a strong competitive advantage right from the start — and still does today, thirty years later. That competitive advantage allowed us not only to survive in a cut-throat business, but eventually to become a market-leader in the region where we operate.

From the beginning, our customer-driven approach

marked us out as a pioneer in our field. It created a national reputation for us as innovators, in spite of the fact that we were then only a very small local operation.

The second thing I found out was that the customer-driven approach that came naturally to me was incredibly rare.

I say "incredibly" because I found it hard to believe that people could so often ignore something that was at the root of their profitability. In those days, *none* of our competitors in Ireland shared our approach — despite the fact that retailing, of all the businesses there are, offers the easiest ways to get close to the customer.

But what has happened now, in the new customer-driven age that we supposedly have arrived at?

Too often, in the US and Europe, customers still feel themselves to be the poor relations.

Too often, in the US as in Europe, excellence in customer service is still hailed as the exception — rather than as the norm.

Why is this?

The reason seems to be that people in business don't know very much about what being customer-driven actually means.

In a nutshell, they don't know *how* to do it.

And therefore, we are in danger of ending up with the worst possible thing: a principle that everyone admits is a winner, a principle that gets lip-service, but a principle that is not acted on.

So my aim with this book is to help you turn that lip-service into action.

17

To do that, I can tell you what being customer-driven means to me, and what I have learned about it in thirty years of running a retailing business.

I can tell you the techniques that have worked for me and how I think they can be made to work in any business.

I can spell out what being customer-driven means for the person at the top of an organization, and for the people who work in it at every level.

What I cannot claim is that becoming customer-driven is easy, because it is not. But I do hope to show you that it is simple — there is nothing terribly complicated about it. This is not a book loaded down with esoteric theory. It is a book about the how, not the why.

Even more important, I also hope to show you that becoming truly customer driven is fun. Being customer-driven is, by a long shot, the most exciting and rewarding way of doing business.

CHAPTER 2

This is where it starts:
The Boomerang Principle

IN THE NEXT FEW PAGES you will find the most important lesson in this book.

It is an umbrella idea that embraces pretty well everything else I believe about being customer driven.

But before explaining what it is, let me tell you how I discovered it.

My first business experience was not in retailing at all, but in the tourism business. In the 1950s my father Eamonn Quinn ran a holiday camp called Red Island, just outside Skerries on the coast of north County Dublin.

Pioneering obviously runs in the Quinn family blood: before going into the holiday business, he had set up and successfully run a chain of retail shops called Payantake that were in many ways the precursors of modern supermarkets. And having blazed a trail there, he moved into the then infant Irish tourism industry with a concept that was very different from the traditional seaside hotel.

I worked at Red Island during my school holidays, doing anything and everything and — though I didn't realize it then — getting an excellent grounding in the basics of customer service. I was a waiter, I was a pageboy, I was a photographer, I was a bingo caller.

But the most important thing I learned was rooted in the particular way the product at Red Island was sold to the customer.

When a customer booked a week or two at Red Island, he paid a bill that included everything. Travel, meals, accommodation, entertainment — everything was included. From the moment the customer arrived, he didn't have to put his hand in his pocket. There were literally no extras.

In those days in particular — just after the Second World War when everything was tight and there wasn't much money around — that all-in-one price was a tremendous attraction. The customers knew exactly where they stood. But what I want to focus on is where it left us.

The fact was that when guests arrived, we had made as much money from their visit as we were going to make. No matter how hard we worked to give them a good time, we would not increase our profit from their stay. That was already fixed.

So why did we work our tails off, week after week, trying to create for these visitors the best holiday experience they had ever had?

The reason was because *we wanted them to come back.* My father wanted to hear people say: "We've had a great time. We're coming back again."

That was the challenge: we wanted them to go away so satisfied with their experience at Red Island that they would be certain to come back the following year.

Every single thing we did was centered on that one overriding aim.

And we had a ready benchmark to judge our success by — the number of repeat bookings. Before many of them left the holiday camp, they paid a deposit for the next year's holiday. Week by week, we had immediate feedback as to how well we'd done — the number of deposits that departing guests put down for the following season.

If it was a good week, we might get perhaps 50 bookings for the next year. If it wasn't a good week, we might only get 12. At the end of each week, we were able to say to each other: "It went well this week." We might not know exactly why, but we would know how we had done. We had an instant barometer of how we had performed in satisfying customers.

As this was my first experience of the world of business, the set-up did not seem in any way unusual to me. Since it was the only thing I knew at the time, I took it as the norm that the right way to run a business was to concentrate on getting people to come back again.

Later, I realized that it was anything but the norm.

Most businesses, after all, do not get their money upfront: how much they take in now depends on how they manage *this* sale, here and now.

And because of this, most businesses focus on the task of maximizing the profit from the current sale. Of course they are interested in repeat business. Who isn't? But they tend to see it as a bonus rather than the main pay-off. And naturally they tend to concentrate on what they see as the main pay-off, with the lesser part of their energy devoted to creating the bonus.

In effect, what they say is: let's look after our profit now, and repeat business will largely look after itself.

My early experience taught me the exact reverse: if you look after getting the repeat business, the profit will largely look after itself.

And this is the first, big lesson in becoming customer-driven:

- **Think of the main task as bringing the customer back.**

That is my Boomerang Principle: the name of the game is getting the customer back.

Once you start to think it through, this principle can radically change the way you do business. At present, your approach may be like playing golf, where the idea is usually to get the ball to travel as far away from you as possible.

When you throw boomerangs, your objective is different, your strategy is different, and the way you judge your results is different.

When we opened our first shop in Dundalk, we almost had to unteach the people who joined us. We had to teach them not to be *too* good as salespeople. They had all been trained in the traditional way.

"A half-pound of bacon, ma'am? Certainly. Hmmm.... It's a bit over. Is that all right?"

In the grocery business, the training was: never go under, always go over.

And yet very quickly, I found that some customers

shopped with us precisely because they preferred to avoid the embarrassment of the slick salesman. They found it difficult to say "no," to admit that they didn't want the bit extra — or that they couldn't afford it.

There was one particular product that we sold an enormous quantity of. It was cheap tea. We sold it at 15 cents a quarter pound. At first we couldn't quite figure out why we did so well with that line.

Brendan Rooney had joined us from Liptons, a big chain then, and he explained that in their counter serviced shops the cheap tea didn't sell at all.

They'd all been instructed, when somebody said, "Could I have a quarter of tea?" to say "Well, will you have the Gold tea at 49 cents, or the Bronze at 39 cents, or the Blue Label at 29 cents? Or, of course, there's always the Black Label at 19 cents."

The mention of the cheapest tea was made with a barely disguised sniff of disdain. Nobody had the temerity to buy the cheapest tea, and Liptons achieved their objective — to get the most from that particular sale.

But in our self-service arrangement, people had no problem choosing exactly the tea that they wanted. They could buy the cheapest tea, if that was what they wanted, with no embarrassment at all.

And as soon as they were offered the opportunity, they took it in a big way. As a result, we gained business — and needless to say, our competitors lost it.

But that was business we would never have had if we had run our operation on the principle of trying to maximize the profit now, rather than concentrating on bringing the customer back for more.

We found the same thing with cheap toilet rolls. We had huge sales, because we were satisfying a latent demand that had been frustrated up to then, demand that had been hidden by embarrassment.

And it was a latent demand that we would never have uncovered if our priority had been to maximize the profit from every sale, in the short term.

We had to teach ourselves, and the new people who joined us as we grew, that being a good salesperson was not getting the customer to buy more, but getting the customer to come back again.

I even got to the point of being torn apart when I considered another part of the traditional grocery training.

Everyone was taught that when a customer asked for a half-pound of bacon, you said:

"Will you have a few sausages and a black pudding to go with that, ma'am?"

I had to think very seriously: given what I believed, should I actually stop them from saying that? Was this not putting a bit of pressure on customers to buy more than they really wanted?

In the end I came to the conclusion that it was no harm to *remind* the customer of the other things that usually went with the product they were buying. That in a sense was an additional customer service.

As I see it, there is a clear dividing line between doing that, and deliberately pushing ten ounces of something at people who have asked for eight.

Sometimes the immediate cost of turning your back on the short-term is very obvious, and the benefit of working for the long-term much less tangible.

An example in our case was our decision to stop stocking candy at the checkouts.

That's a profitable way to sell candy, because it caters for the impulse purchase. But we found, through our customer panels, that it also caused a lot of hassle for mothers shopping with young children.

While the mother was stopped at the checkout, the child was faced with a tantalizing selection of goodies — and would often kick up blue murder until the mother bought some peace with something from the candy display.

In response to this criticism, we began to keep one checkout in each shop free of candy.

The customer reaction was immediate and highly positive — so much so that we became convinced the only practical way to continue the scheme was to extend it to all the checkouts.

This decision tested our customer-driven commitment.

Because on the one hand we had hard figures that detailed the business we were about to forego. On the other hand, we were not able to quantify the benefit that we would achieve by making the change.

We felt sure that eventually the benefit would be greater than the cost, but we had no way of telling in a way that would satisfy an accountant. And we had to admit that we would never be able to pin down the benefits so precisely that we could *prove* that the change was beneficial.

A similar example was our playhouses for small children.

Again, our customer panels revealed that mothers shopping with young children had a major problem. The customer had difficulty concentrating on the serious business of shopping while coping with children under her feet.

I remember well the day I first became convinced we had to do something about minding our customers' children.

A group of customers, all young mothers, were talking about the improvement in their shopping pleasure since we had removed candy from the checkout.

"It's the reason I come past two other supermarkets," said one mother.

"You see, I have three-year-old twin boys and I have to take a Valium every day to cope with them. But on the day I come shopping, I take three Valium! It's hell trying to control them in a supermarket.

"If only you could do something about that, I'd be a loyal customer for life."

We found there were very many others like her. But the customers with children were not the only ones with a problem. Other customers found it a hassle to have other people's children under their feet.

Out of this came the idea for the Superquinn playhouses, which have long been one of our most famous trademarks. We got into them because of the Boomerang Principle: we wanted to provide a service that would give people a reason for coming back to shop with us, rather than going to our competitors.

In doing this, we were incurring a major cost — a cost that was easily quantified. We started in a modest way, with mobile playbuses that toured the different shops, spending one day a week at each. But customer demand for the service meant that we soon had to consider providing permanent playhouses at each shop.

This meant employing specialist staff, it meant providing valuable space, it meant buying equipment. It represented both a one-time cost and a continuing drain on our resources — both of which were easy to quantify.

What was less easy to quantify were the benefits. In fact, let's be honest about it. The benefits were *impossible* to quantify in hard figures. Certainly in advance, and even in retrospect. However, we took both these decisions. We removed candy from all our checkouts. And we provided playhouses at all our shops. Several years later, I am fully convinced that both decisions have paid off handsomely.

I am in no doubt at all that in terms of building customer loyalty — in helping us get our customers to come back to us — the benefits have greatly outweighed the costs.

But make no mistake about it: you sometimes need considerable courage to take the unquantifiable option. This is where *leadership* comes in.

The person at the top of the business must sometimes be prepared to put his or her neck on the line because of a hunch, a gut instinct.

Sometimes the role of the leader is to say to the others:

"All right, we can't show this with figures. But I am prepared to take the long view, and my instinct is that we will benefit more in the long run from doing such-and-such."

This is what business risk is all about. And, of course, if you want to stay in business your instincts had better be *right*.

An important part of becoming *successfully* customer-driven is honing your instincts so that they give you the right answers most of the time, and all of the time when a decision is critical to the future of the business.

The stakes are high, but to encourage you, let me give you a glance at the benefits. Sometimes, when you budget for an immediate cost against a long term less tangible benefit, you end up getting a pleasant surprise.

Sometimes the dividend comes much sooner than you expect.

For example, I was chairman of the Irish postal service when it went semi-state as An Post in 1984. We were anxious to make a big splash — to grab the public's attention right at the start, and bring home to them that here was a completely new ball-game.

Our idea for this was a one-day return of the "Penny Post." In the 19th century that was what it cost to post a letter — one penny. We decided that anyone posting a hand-addressed letter on the first day of the new An Post could do so at a cost of only one penny.

We restricted it to hand-addressed post to avoid being taken advantage of by people with mass-mailings. But even so, the promotion had a certain cost. We worked out what it would be and decided to invest in it as a business-builder for the future.

What actually happened, to our surprise, was that the promotion paid for itself.

The "Penny Post" was dramatically successful. It was highly popular with the general public, and people got out pen and paper who hadn't done so for years.

Literally *millions* of letters were posted at the give-away rate, and we lost every bit as much as we anticipated.

However, many of the people who had been written to at the penny rate replied to the letters they had received. And their replies went at the full rate!

So when we looked at the business for the week or two in question, we discovered that the launch promotion had covered its costs within the short term — even though it had been conceived of as a long-term investment.

The Boomerang Principle has worked well for me and the businesses I have been connected with. But why should you be in the boomerang business?

Because all trading operations, not just retailing ones, depend mainly on repeat business for their profitability.

They depend on it particularly for their growth.

All trading operations?

Yes, I believe so.

If you are tempted to doubt that proposition, here is a challenge.

Put into the box on the next page all the trading activities you can think of that definitely do not in the long run depend on repeat business.

Spend a few minutes thinking about it, and see what

29

you can write in the box.

But before you write, think it through.

Are you really sure the operation does not depend on repeat business?

Really sure?

Really?

Is it still empty?

I would be very surprised if it is not.

Often when I put this challenge to people, they offer the business of funeral undertakers as the perfect exception. That's a service you use only once, right? But of course it's not an exception at all.

Those who buy an undertaker's service are not the dead, but the living. And as any undertaker will tell you, in making their sad decision the buyers of funeral services are usually very much influenced by a previous relationship they had with an undertaking firm — even though it may have been many years before.

Another, more promising candidate for an exception is the one-time rip-off merchants who prey on customers unlikely ever to travel that way again. Such operations certainly do exist in many parts of the world; we have all experienced them at one time or other.

Some of them may indeed be genuine exceptions to my rule, but how many businesses want to model themselves on that?

One of the reasons why very few of us would be prepared to build a business on making the sale no matter what is because we realize the importance of *reputation*. Existing customers can either bring back business themselves, or they can create new business for us by *referral*.

This is an absolutely vital way of growing your business, but it tends to get less than its fair share of attention from marketing people because creating referrals is not something that you can do with conventional "marketing tools" — it is entirely a matter of how you run your business.

After we had decided to run our business on the Boomerang Principle we then extended that challenge a step further. We started to ask ourselves:

"First we have to get that customer coming back. Then when we've made sure of that, we have to do whatever it takes to get her to recommend us to her next-door neighbors. What do we have to do to make that happen?

"What do we have to do so that when she goes home she talks to the people who live next door to her, about her shopping experience? To get her talking about us with such enthusiasm that her neighbors are encouraged to give us a try?"

It helps to picture that situation, to imagine it happening. That makes it easier to imagine what you have to do to *make* it happen.

Reputation is, of course, two-sided. Just as people can recommend you to their friends, they can do the opposite.

A dissatisfied customer can do two things, both of which are disastrous for you.

Of the two, the lesser disaster is that the customer does not come back. The bigger disaster is that he or she will talk about their dissatisfaction and turn off other potential customers.

The ultimate fate of many rip-off merchants is that potential new customers get warned off by people who have already been stung. In the meantime, certainly, some of them may grow rich — but that is hardly a recipe for sustained growth and profitability.

All of this illustrates just how far we have to stretch before finding an example of a business that does not depend on repeat business.

Maybe not all, but by far the overwhelming majority of operations *do* depend on their customers coming back, and *do* depend on their customers making favorable referrals.

And yet, most businesses do *not* approach the marketplace on that assumption. Most people in business set out to play golf, rather than to throw boomerangs.

I am not accusing them of being out for a quick killing; what I am saying is that their priorities are usually focused around the profits that come in the short term, rather than on the long-term dividends that can result from a continuing customer relationship.

All too often, the real energy on the marketing front goes into attracting new customers, while the ultimately more important task of nourishing the existing customer base gets a lower glamour rating.

Don't get me wrong: obviously attracting new customers directly (not just through referral) is very important, and most businesses have to do it. But most of us simply cannot afford to buy all our customers in this way, week after week or month after month.

The cost is *always* too high, if the only payback from marketing costs are the immediate sale. On the other hand, when that cost is a first investment in a continuing profitable relationship — then it makes sound business sense.

What doesn't seem to make sense is investing heavily to attract the customer in the first place, then failing to match that effort with the follow-through that creates the long-term relationship.

The reason why we too often fail to match the marketing effort with follow-through is because we get bewitched by short-term payoffs. Because they are the easiest to measure, we are tempted to measure them alone.

And what we measure, we do something about.

What we don't measure, gets put on the back burner unless leadership from a customer-driven top person changes the priorities.

Somehow or other, you have to find ways of measuring customer satisfaction. This is much harder than it sounds. For instance, you won't measure customer satisfaction by counting the number of complaints you get. That, as I'll explain later, could be a highly misleading measure.

One area that's worth looking at is measuring the speed of response of your organization. I came across an idea recently at an American airport that impressed me, and at the moment I'm working out how to adapt it to our operation.

An enormous egg-timer sat at the check-in desk of a car rental firm. A notice beside it said:

"Set the timer going. If we haven't served you by the time the sand runs out, you get your first day's rental free."

This did a number of things all at once.

First of all, it got over to me, the customer, that this was an organization that recognized the importance of speed to the customer at the other side of the counter. When you've spent several hours sitting on a plane, you want to get moving straight away. The egg-timer signalled that they realized that.

Second, it provided something concrete for the counter staff to measure their performance against. Responding quickly is something that they knew was important, but without the timer the aspiration to perform well could very easily slip.

Worse, without the timer they could fool themselves into thinking that all that was important was to get an acceptable average of prompt responses. Forgetting that the one customer who has to wait a long time outweighs in importance many, many others who have had no problem.

And third, the timer introduced an element of fun into the dreary routine of checking in for a car rental. As we'll see later, fun is highly important in the fight for competitive advantage — and it's a factor that you only appreciate when you learn to see customers as people, not as statistics.

So look for ways to measure customer satisfaction — as many as you can. At Red Island all those years ago, we were fortunate. The only thing we needed to measure once the season had begun was our success in getting deposits on repeat bookings.

That focused our attention in the right place, concentrating our minds on the job that needed to be done.

It paid off for both us and our customers, because what produced results for *them* produced results for us.

There was no conflict of interest, as there could have been if we had had an interest in getting them to spend more for our short-term benefit.

And that is one of the beauties of the Boomerang Principle: if you apply it, you and the customer are *on the same side*.

You want the customer to come back, and the only way you can make sure of that is by keeping the customer satisfied. So the relationship with your customer is not an adversary one; it is a partnership.

Does this mean you ignore the short-term return altogether?

Of course not.

There is no point in having your heart in the right place if you can't get your sums right. More specifically, there is no point in investing in the future if you're not going to be in business to reap the harvest from that investment.

What the Boomerang Principle offers is a way of setting priorities.

The normal way is to put the short-term result ahead of the longer-term relationship; under the Boomerang Principle, you reverse that priority. But both elements are still important.

How do you put that principle into effect? Most of the rest of this book is about ways of doing that. Almost everything I have to say is geared to getting customers to come back for more. But right away, here are three steps towards making it a reality:

- **First**, when faced with any business decision, any call on your time or resources, get in the habit of asking: *What will this do to help bring the customer back again?*

If the answer is "not much," then ask whether you should be doing it at all. But if the answer is "a lot," then you can be a lot surer that you are on the right track. And you should not be too worried about getting a full return on your investment right away.

- **Second**, set up ways of measuring how much repeat and referral business you get.

  It's amazing how many less useful statistics businesses will generate, while ignoring these key indicators.

  Remember: what gets measured, gets action. What isn't measured, gets ignored.

- **Third**, admit that sometimes in choosing between the short-term and the long-term benefits, you will need courage to take the option whose benefits may be hard to quantify.

  Be ready to exercise that courage, while appreciating that you are now depending on your instincts — and you now have a very good reason to set about sharpening those instincts.

How do you sharpen the instincts that will help you towards the right decisions? By getting a *feel* for the customer.

Crowning the Customer

CHAPTER 3

Getting a "feel" for the customer

BECOMING CUSTOMER-DRIVEN IS, above all, a question of getting closer to the customer than people in business usually are.

Why?

Because to make the decisions that will bring your customers back, you need to think like a customer.

You need to be able to wear the customer's hat, to walk in their shoes.

You need to get a "feel" for the customer.

In a real sense, you need to be able to *become* a customer.

Few people realize just how difficult this is. In retailing we call it "jumping the counter." Your business may not have counters between you and your customers, but the principle is the same.

The marketplace looks totally different from where the customer is standing.

In our business, we have a rule which requires our top management to do their own household shopping once a month. This gives them first-hand experience of what shopping is like, seen from the customer's perspective.

First-hand is crucial. I remember one of my executives saying to me:

"There's no need for me to do that. My wife does the shopping, and she tells me exactly what is going on."

He had missed the point. The customer perspective is something that you have to experience *for yourself.*

When *you've* stood in a line for four minutes at a time when you're under pressure to get away and do something else, you discover just how long four minutes can be. You see the problem of waiting in a very different light to the one you have when looking at it from the management perspective.

I mention lines in particular because one thing that I have learned from staying close to the customer is that everyone is now much more time-conscious than they once were.

This is a long-term trend that has developed slowly. You have to be particularly alert to be able to spot such trends.

If you respond to the customer by the norms of 20 years ago, you risk missing the boat.

Being your own customer on a regular basis is something that you must do to become customer-driven.

How you do it will vary according to your business: you identify the points at which your customer has contact with your company and try to experience what they experience.

Even phoning your own switchboard can be a eye-opening experience. You also get a very good picture of how long your customers are kept waiting for a reply. You get a very good idea of the initial impression that your company makes on the phone.

So if you have to call your office, make sure that you dial the call yourself. You may learn something. And if you don't ring your office regularly, find an excuse for doing so!

A word of warning: you may need to work hard to avoid having yourself treated as a VIP.

This is precisely what you do not want. Most of your customers are not treated as VIPs. The perspective you want is that of the ordinary customer.

There's a certain airline that I travel with quite frequently, and it always amuses me to see how management from the airline get priority treatment from the cabin staff when they travel as passengers. It's not just that I, as a paying customer, feel that the cabin staff's attention should be focused on me and people like me.

What really amuses me about the situation is that I can see how inaccurate a picture these people are getting of what it is like to travel on their airline.

But just to show you that I don't think I am perfect myself in this regard, let me tell you about something that happened recently in our company that really shocked me when I learned about it.

Every Thursday morning, in every Superquinn shop, a member of top management comes around with the previous week's figures. I do this just like the others.

We spend a number of hours going around each department in the shop. We talk over the figures with the staff, show them how their department is doing against their target, against the same week the previous year, against similar departments in other shops, and against other departments in the same shop.

This is a vital part of our effort to work as a team.

41

Everybody can see how their efforts have paid off, and how they fit in to the big picture.

After I had done the figures in one of our shops recently, I was on the way out and stopped to greet a number of customers and pass the time of day with them as I usually do.

But one of the customers, a man, was clearly exasperated when he returned my greeting.

"Ah, don't be talking," he said. "It was all your fault I was kept waiting round here twenty minutes today. All because of you and your pep-talk!"

I hadn't a clue what he was talking about at first. But it emerged that he had come to have a birthday cake inscribed with a personalized message — something we do as a customer service, and which takes just a minute or two of a baker's time.

But that day, because I was talking about the figures to the bakers, one of the counter staff must have said to him:

"All the bakers are busy at the moment, they're talking to Feargal Quinn. Could you hold on for about ten or fifteen minutes?"

That's an example of where the customer didn't come first. *The boss came first.* And that should never happen.

Yet I had allowed it to happen, by not looking at my talks with the staff from the customer's perspective.

Why is it so vitally important to stand in the customer's shoes?

Because if you are in the business of serving the customer, as we all are, there are two big temptations that can throw you off course.

The first temptation is to run the operation to suit yourself, not the customers. Giving into this temptation can be fatal for a business.

Sometimes what the customer needs is very inconvenient, and the knee jerk reaction can be to avoid giving it to them.

Sometimes the people who are meant to be competing for the customer's business get together and agree *not* to give the customer what they want.

In my career in retailing, some of the best examples of this temptation in action have had to do with opening hours.

When I went into business first, for instance, it was the custom in the grocery trade in Dublin for shops to close on Wednesday afternoons. There was no evening shopping at all.

We soon realized that this cozy arrangement between retailers was not what the customers wanted.

Their lifestyles were changing, and the shops that were meant to be serving them were not keeping up. This created a vacuum in the marketplace, and therefore an opportunity for us.

We decided to open not when it suited the grocery trade to open, but when it suited the customer. Very quickly others were forced to follow us, and what had seemed to be "unchangeable" became no longer so.

Some people did not like this, and indeed some firms went out of business because they tried to hold on to the old ways for too long.

This is the terrifying side of yielding to the temptation to suit yourself, not the customer: you may put yourself out of business.

43

This temptation is not confined just to the people who run businesses. It is a disease that can affect *everyone* who works in a business, and one that can put the strategy of trade unions in a tragically self-destructive direction.

Again from my own experience, I remember a time when bakers in Dublin decided to turn their back on the customer and suit themselves instead.

To bake fresh bread each day, bakers need to start work very early in the morning. Few people like doing this, but for generations it had been accepted as a part of a baker's life.

Then the bakers got together and decided to do it a different way. They would work "normal" hours, and the customer who shopped in the morning would have to put up with bread that had been baked the previous day.

The customers did "put up" with it, but they did not like it.

And the inevitable eventually happened: someone found a means of breaking this cartel, and giving the customer what they did want.

Bakeries in the country outside Dublin leapt into the gap, and trucked their bread into the capital to compete with the local produce. (To do this, the country bakers had to start work even earlier in the morning!)

And some supermarket chains, like our own, started baking their own bread, right inside the shop where the customer could see and smell it being baked — providing the best evidence that it was really fresh.

Many of the bakeries who tried to turn their back on

the customer are no longer in business today. The people who ran them did not have a *feel* for the customer, and neither did the people who worked in them nor their trade unions.

They learned this lesson the hard way:

If you don't run your business to suit your customers, your customers will suit themselves — in the long run.

Obviously, you may have to do *some* things that customers don't want in order to keep your costs within limits.

Setting out to please all of the people all the time may be just as much a recipe for disaster as ignoring the customer's wishes altogether.

But the customer-driven business is the one that always says "Why not?" rather than "No, we couldn't because..."

Get into the habit of saying "Why not?" rather than rushing into a negative judgement. You will be surprised to find how often the impractical turns out to be quite do-able.

The second big temptation that gets between us and our customers is to think that we know the customer very well.

We don't.

And we never will.

The best we can hope to do is to keep increasing our knowledge of the customer, all the time.

But we fool ourselves if we think we will ever know our marketplace well enough to be able to tell in advance exactly how the customers will react to what we do.

I can think of a very good example of this.

Some time after we introduced salad bars in our shops, I was standing by the salad bar in one of the shops quite late in the evening. A customer, who happened to be Swiss, said to me in exasperation:

"Look at this display. It's terrible. All the trays are nearly empty."

"Ah," I said. "Let me explain why.

"You see, we pride ourselves in never selling anything from the day before. So as the evening comes, we let the stock run down a little — we don't keep on making new salads that would be left over until the morning.

"If one runs out, of course, we replace it immediately — but if we kept the trays full there would be lots of fresh salads left over. So the way the display looks is actually a demonstration of our 'only fresh today' policy."

But the customer was having none of that.

"But it looks terrible!"

We had put the emphasis on freshness, and had accepted the half-empty trays in the evening as the inevitable price that had to be paid in order to achieve that freshness. We had to choose between one thing or the other.

Right?

As it happened, no.

In thirty seconds, the customer explained what he would do.

"When a tray gets half-full, put it into a smaller tray. And when that gets half-full, put it into an even smaller one. That way you won't have your leftovers, but the display will look attractive because the trays will always be full ."

This is so simple and basic that I am almost ashamed to tell you about it.

The important thing is that we could not see it. We had thought that our customers would appreciate what we were doing about freshness, and would accept the trade-off.

But this customer's actual reaction was quite different.

Reactions to what you communicate to customers are notoriously difficult to forecast. Only experience teaches you that anything can be misunderstood.

For instance, we have always given away bones for customers' dogs, and at one stage we decided to put up a sign reminding people about it. It was attractively designed with a cartoon character, and it said:

WOOF !

Take home some bones for your dog.

I never thought about it again until one day at a customer panel, a shopper said:

"No, I don't shop here for my meat. I go to the butchers down the road, because they give me free bones for my dog."

"But they do that here," the other customers chorused.

"We even have a sign about it," I added diffidently, wondering to myself about how to communicate with people who never read signs.

"Oh, I saw the sign," she said. "But it never said the

bones were free."

She was quite right. It had never crossed our minds that we needed to say "free," because it had never crossed our minds to charge for them.

Of course we didn't: *nobody* charged for bones. We made the mistake of assuming that we didn't need to say they were free; we thought that nobody would think we were trying to sell them.

We were wrong.

In truth, I am not ashamed at all to tell you about obvious mistakes like these. Because I believe that the truly customer-driven are the people:

- who admit that they don't know everything (or nearly everything) there is to know about their customers;
- who acknowledge that they can't forecast precisely how their customers will react, and;
- who are committed to a lifelong effort to remedy that gap in their knowledge — to keep narrowing the gap, rather than widening it.

Do I hear you saying:

"But hold on a minute! Isn't this what the techniques of market research are for? Surely these sophisticated tools can tell us all we want to know?"

Not so.

Formal market research is *not* enough.

Mind you, it is essential. No business that hopes to grow in a changing marketplace can afford to neglect the use of market research. The trend towards spending more money on research, and researching more things in more depth than ever before is in my view a correct one.

48

But no matter how much we invest in formal research, we must not fool ourselves that it will ever give us a *feel* for the customer. And what marks out the customer-driven business is that *feel*.

There are many things that market research won't tell you; things that I believe to be essential. Let me spell out just one of them:

Market research will rarely uncover the minority of one who is right.

What market research is pre-eminently good at is revealing the balance of opinions and preferences.

You may be aware of a niche in the market, for instance, and research can put numbers on it: it can tell you whether there is a market in the niche.

What market research is not so good at is identifying the individual opinion that seems to go against the tide, but which is sometimes the signal for a major opportunity or the warning of a major problem.

Here's an example from my own experience.

In our early days at Superquinn, we identified a customer need for personal service when buying meat. In the 1960s, if you wanted personal service you went to a butcher shop; if you wanted a lower price, you bought your meat from a self-service display in a supermarket.

We recognized that very many customers preferred the personal butcher service, so we decided to provide it within the framework of a supermarket. (This is old hat now, but it was a novel idea then.)

Instead of the refrigerated cabinets of pre-packed meat bought in from outside, we employed real butchers.

49

They cut up their meat within view of the customer and were available to give the customer advice on what to buy and how to cook it.

This was a dramatic success.

It became one of the foundations of our reputation for superior personal service to our customers.

It was the first step towards what eventually became a full range of staffed "shops within the shop" that included fish counters, bakeries, customized pizza counters, sausage counters, and so on.

It was also highly profitable. It brought us a lot of trade that up to then had bypassed supermarkets altogether.

Nevertheless, it was something that we continued to research carefully. We had, of course, flown in the face of a long-term world trend — we were moving back from self-service to personal service, while the world seemed to be going the opposite way.

Were we trying to buck an inevitable trend, and did we run the danger of eventually being left high and dry with an outmoded means of selling?

Because of this, year after year we kept asking our customers, in a variety of different ways: is this what you like?

Do you really prefer the butcher service to the self-service displays?

Every time we asked the question, by whatever technique and in whatever forum, we got the same overwhelming response:

Butcher service is what we want. It's terrific, keep it up.

I remember one customer panel in particular where I brought the issue up. I'll cover our customer panels in more detail later, but for the moment let me just say that these are groups of about 12 volunteer shoppers, who sit down with me regularly and talk about their shopping experiences with us.

My question about the butcher service was a regular one for these groups, and on this occasion I got the by now usual response:

It's great, keep it up. Don't dream of going pre-pack like the other supermarkets.

There was just a single dissenter among that group. She was not so enthusiastic about the butcher service.

She said:

"Actually, I shouldn't be here at all, I just came here with Mrs. Doyle. I don't shop here much, and I never buy my meat here. You see, down at the other supermarket I can rummage through the pre-pack display until I find a lamb-chop or a steak that suits my pocket — the sort of thing I can afford."

Hers was very much a minority view. And before I could open my mouth, the rest of the group disagreed with her.

They didn't have that difficulty, they insisted.

Sure, you didn't know exactly how much it was going to cost — but the butchers were very good at cutting the amount you wanted. If you asked for a pound of steak, you might end up with an ounce or two more, but that was it. It wasn't really a problem at all.

And even if it was a slight problem, the other advantages of the butcher service far outweighed it. *Don't take it away from us, Feargal!*

Well, the group certainly succeeded in shutting the

51

customer up. We heard no more about the objection, and we moved on to other things.

But when I reviewed the meeting afterwards with my colleagues, the problem raised by that single customer continued to nag at me. The fact was that she did not buy her meat from us. For what to her was an excellent reason. How many other people like her were there?

Despite all our probings, we had no idea. We had consistently been asking the same questions:

Do you prefer the butcher service? Would you like us to do self-service instead, like the others?

Again and again we had got the same answer. And even in the free-ranging customer panels, no-one had ever made this comment to us.

Statistically, that comment was insignificant. The logical side of me was tempting me to ignore it. But my instincts about our marketplace — this *feel* for the customer that I have been talking about — prevented me from dismissing it.

So I decided to carry out a little experiment.

In just one of our shops, and on a temporary basis, we put in a small refrigerated display directly across the way from our butcher counter. We filled it not with factory-packed meat but with meat cut by our own butchers, of exactly the same quality and price. But every pack was, of course, marked with the exact price that the customer had to pay.

We did this with some misgivings. For years we had positioned ourselves as the supermarket with personal butcher service. We knew that customers saw this as one of the main differences between ourselves and the other supermarkets.

That was why we had never put in the refrigerated displays when we created our butcher service. And why, incidentally, we had always approached this question on an "either/or" basis.

But would the appearance of a refrigerated display weaken the clear image that we had projected? Would our customers see it as the beginning of the end?

That was why we dipped our toes in the water so tentatively. We wanted to be able to pull back quickly if the reaction was negative.

Well, we put in the display in our Northside shop and waited for the results. They were nothing short of astounding.

The sales from our butcher counter remained totally unchanged. But sales from the refrigerated display immediately took off, to the extent that within six weeks *we had doubled our entire sales of meat in that shop.*

Clearly, that lone dissenting customer at the panel discussion was not alone. Far from it. She was alone in that she had the courage to speak out against the tide, and to voice an opinion that we had never heard before and didn't know how to probe for.

Interestingly, once we had the choice in place, our customers found all kinds of reasons to use the refrigerated display — ones that had never come up before.

For instance, people found it convenient when they wanted to buy just a single piece of meat. It was faster than going to the butcher, and maybe having to wait their turn to be served.

The main point here is how *obvious* this solution looks with hindsight. Reading it, you may have thought: how could they have been so stupid not to see that opportunity?

Why did they never think of providing the two options, instead of thinking of it as an "either/or" choice?

Obvious it may have been, but we did not see it.

Nor did most of our customers.

And we would never have seen it if we had gone on making our decisions about selling meat just by counting heads.

In this case, the minority of one was right.

And market research, whether quantitative or qualitative, will rarely tell you much about the minority of one.

Here are three of the many other things that market research won't do:

- Market research won't communicate to you the mood of your customers, or the tone of their relationship with you.
  Those you have to experience for yourself.

- Market research won't directly confront you with criticism, which is a highly salutary experience. Sure, research can tell you when you have erred, but when you are looking at that conclusion on an impersonal sheet of paper, you can kid yourself into being philosophical about it. It's quite a different matter to find out about your mistakes through direct confrontation with a

customer who suffers the consequences. When
you experience the emotional strength of a
customer's reaction, you are much more likely to
do something about it — believe me.

• Perhaps most important, market research won't
  communicate to you the ideas that your customers have for your business.
  I have found customers to be a most valuable
  source of good business ideas — but I have also
  found that the only way to elicit those ideas is
  through direct dialogue.

To sum up the lesson of this chapter: getting
customers to come back again and again depends
critically on your ability to develop a *feel* for the
customer.

It's a feel that can never be achieved through indirect
means such as market research.

You can achieve it only through *direct personal*
contact with the customers who generate your
business.

CHAPTER 4

*Listening to customers:
the first big secret*

NOW LET'S LOOK A LITTLE MORE CLOSELY
at what direct personal contact with the customer
means.

How do you go about it?

How do you make it part of your business life, day
in and day out?

The key to direct personal contact with customers is
listening.

If you can learn to listen effectively to your
customers, all the rest will follow, almost
automatically.

*The single most important skill you need to become truly
customer-driven is the ability to listen.*

But there is a problem here.

"Listening to your customers" is a cliché nowadays.
You have been told to do it many times. Perhaps you
feel that you have already put this advice into effect.

Many organizations, in fact, are so confident about
their listening ability that they have made the claim to
be good listeners into a plank of their advertising
platform.

In my experience, however, the organizations that
truly listen, as opposed to the ones who claim to do
so, are few and far between. The business people who
can truly listen, as opposed to the ones who claim to
do so, are almost as rare.

What we have here, once again, is widespread recognition of the value of a sound business principle, and widespread failure to put that principle into action! It's the "lip-service syndrome."

The result is that listening still offers the individual business person, and the individual company, an excellent opportunity to steal a march on their competitors.

One of the reasons why this opportunity still exists is because listening to customers is very hard to do.

Very hard indeed.

And the proof is that so few people in business do it well.

In my experience there are three big secrets to effective listening. Experiment with them, and I am sure you will find your listening skills improve.

Here is listening secret No. 1:

Put in a listening system, and work it

You need a *system* for listening to your customers.

If you don't have a system, listening will remain just an aspiration.

Sure, you can resolve to listen more to your customers. When you go to work tomorrow, you will put that resolution into effect. And the first day, because it is foremost in your mind, you will listen.

But the second day you will listen less, because other priorities will start to fight for your attention.

And the third day you will listen even less.

And so on, until within a very short time your determination to listen more to your customers has gone the way of all well-intentioned resolutions.

So *don't* resolve to listen more.

Resolve instead to build a system for better listening, for yourself or for your organization.

That way you will have concrete objectives, which can be made into a routine and which stand a far better chance of becoming a permanent part of the way you do business — a permanent part of your strategy for achieving competitive advantage and growth.

Our listening system in Superquinn is a major contributor to our success. Apart from the thousands of minor things it tells us from day-to-day, it is particularly valuable as an early-warning system.

Through it we become aware of changing trends among our customers, ahead of the opposition. We tend to hear about emerging trends much earlier than others. This early warning has, again and again, given us the opportunity to be the first in the field.

The biggest single example of this that I can think of is the trend towards *freshness* that developed in the early 1970s.

Before that there had been a long-term trend towards convenience in foods: goods that were conveniently packaged, and easy to prepare.

This had overlapped into how fresh goods were sold. Fruit and vegetables, for instance, tended increasingly to be-prepacked and sold by the package rather than by weight.

Then, almost imperceptibly at first, customer priorities changed. We suddenly discovered, through our listening system, that freshness was now becoming much more important than before.

In particular, customers were developing a preference towards handling the produce.

I remember well the day this came home to me. I asked a customer at the checkout what she thought of our new mineolas (an unusual kind of orange). She replied that she hadn't noticed because she did not usually shop for her fruit with us.

"You see, I like to handle the fruit before I buy it, and you have it all wrapped up in little packs."

She was overheard by the customer beside her who joined in with similar comments, and then by another customer and another. I discovered that a high proportion of our customers were not buying their fruit and vegetables from us anymore, and there I was on the shop floor surrounded by half a dozen of them, telling me:

"The little shop down the road still sells them loose, and we much prefer it that way."

With that early warning, we were the first supermarket to do away with the packaged selling of produce – replacing them with displays where customers were able to select their own.

It was a response that paid off on the bottom line: our sales of fresh fruit and vegetables went up, because it won back sales that had been drifting away — not to other supermarkets, but to the more traditional kind of shops that had always allowed customers to choose in this way.

In the longer term, it gave a further impetus to our development of the wide variety of fresh food counters which is our main speciality today.

What was of importance to us, of course, was that we were ahead of the competition in our own market. But interestingly, we later discovered that there was a worldwide trend in the same direction — and we had been ahead of that, too.

A later trend that we were also able to spot early on was the increasing importance of healthy eating to our customers.

Within a very short period, healthy eating moved out of what had been a narrow niche and came right into the mainstream. This profoundly affected almost everything we did in our shops and in one area, salad bars, gave rise to a completely new product line.

Later still, we became aware much earlier than our competitors of the developing strength of our customers' feelings about the environment — concerns like the ozone layer, the pollution problems created by certain kinds of packaging and so on.

While others read about these issues in the newspapers or in dry research reports, we were getting it stronger and earlier directly from our shop floor.

Another advantage of bottom line importance that our listening system gave us was an awareness that, increasingly, customers found the passage through the checkouts the most stressful part of shopping.

It was as a direct result of that awareness that we introduced bag-packers at our checkouts. It's a customer service that we have found is enough in itself to get some customers to come back to us week after week.

As far back as the 1960s in our Finglas branch, I

remember a customer leaving the shop saying to me:

"You know, I pass *five* other shops to come here just because you have somebody to pack my bags at the very point in my shopping when I am most tense — the checkout! The other shops leave me on my own to worry about both the bill and the packing."

Even now, our listening system provides us with constant guidance as to how our customers want their bags packed.

We started off thinking it was a fairly simple thing — just a matter of keeping smelly things like soaps and washing powders well away from food, of making sure you didn't pack heavy things in on top of tomatoes, and so on.

In fact, we have found through our listening system that packing bags to the full satisfaction of customers is a very involved process. It's not an exaggeration to say that we learn something new about it every day.

That's the kind of valuable hands-on guidance that a listening system provides.

So what does a listening system look like?

To illustrate, let's take a walk through the system we use in our business.

The first thing about a listening system is that it should have *several* different elements.

You should resist the temptation to rely exclusively, or even mainly, on one listening channel.

The reason is that no listening channel, however effective, can tell you the whole story. It will be biased in some way. That bias is only a problem if you are unaware of it, or if you fail to compensate for it.

Let me give you an example. One of the most

important listening channels I use is customer panels.

These are regular meetings with small groups of volunteer customers. I sit down with them for a meeting that lasts perhaps 90 minutes, and in that time I never fail to learn something new about our business.

Customer panels are so valuable that I strongly recommend you consider creating their equivalent in your business, and in chapter 7 I give some practical hints on how to go about it.

But customer panels on their own are not enough. Why?

Because they are biased, like any listening channel inevitably is.

For one thing, they consist only of our own customers. They are people who have decided to shop with us, more or less regularly. So they do not include people who prefer to shop elsewhere — either people who have never shopped with us, or people who may have once shopped with us but now do so somewhere else.

To get those perspectives, we have to do other research.

Another built-in bias is that customer panels consist mainly of people who generally approve of the way we do things. They like us at least to the extent that they are prepared to give up 90 minutes of their time without payment, to help us run our business better They are generally people who are "on our side" already.

Biases like these do not make a listening channel useless — far from it. But they make any individual listening channel very dangerous if you rely on it exclusively, to get your feel of the marketplace.

Here are just some of the listening channels that we use in our business:

- customer panels;
- customer comment forms;
- customer service desks;
- handling customer complaints positively;
- inviting customer inquiries directly to staff;
- managerial staff accessible to customers;
- formal market research,
- media comment.

The number of separate listening channels we use may seem overwhelming. But in fact they all complement each other, adding up to a rounded picture that we could not get by using a more restricted approach.

Given that we have a comprehensive system of customer panels, why do we bother with customer comment forms?

Because some customers want a way to communicate their views to us quickly, or perhaps without revealing who they are.

Many of the comments duplicate what we hear at the customer panels, but some of them do not — more than enough to make the exercise worthwhile.

Given that we have both customer panels and customer comment forms, why do we feel the need to have customer service desks in every store as well?

These desks offer immediate contact for a comment or a problem, but in a personalized way.

Just as there are people who don't want to make a

comment or a complaint face-to-face and therefore
welcome the anonymity of a customer comment
form, equally there are people who look on writing as
a hassle and who would much prefer to have a few
words with a sympathetic person.

Why do we look on customer complaints as an
important listening channel?

Because complaints are the safety-valve of our
business — and indeed, of any business.

We work on the assumption that for every person
who complains, there are perhaps a dozen who do
not. The dozen who do not are people who will take
their business elsewhere, or who — even more
damagingly — will talk about their bad experience to
other people.

So we regard complaints not only as important
matters in themselves, but as highly valuable
indicators of things we must fix. (More about this in
chapter 8.)

You'll already get the picture that customers in
Superquinn have a variety of ways in which they can
communicate with us and in which we can listen to
them. But we are not at the end of the road yet.

Apart from the customer panels, the customer
comment forms, the customer service desks, the
positive approach to complaints, we also consistently
encourage our customers to talk to *anyone* in the store.

Our floor staff wear sweaters bearing the invitation
"May I help you?" At each department, we have
signs that identify the person in charge of that
department and encourage the customers to consult
them about any query they have.

We do this for three reasons.

First, because we want to make dialogue with customers a feature of the whole shopping experience — not something that customers have to go to a special place to do, or seek out special people for.

Second, because we believe that most queries and problems are best dealt with by the people most directly concerned.

And third, we do it because we want everybody in the shop listening to customers — not just a select few.

We work on the basis that an important part of *everybody's* job is listening to customers.

The truly customer-driven organization is one in which everyone listens.

Everybody includes the managers. Though most problems can be dealt with by other people, there are always some things that people would prefer to see the manager about.

And of course, it's vitally important that the managers themselves keep in close contact with their customers.

That is why we aim to make them as accessible as possible to the customers: for much of the time, they are out there on the shop floor — highly visible, highly approachable, and providing yet another channel of communication between our customers and our company.

There are more indirect listening channels, too.

We monitor press comments about Superquinn quite carefully. It often provides useful insights, and can be valuable when taken in conjunction with what we are hearing through other channels.

What is really valuable is hostile or adverse comment, and you have to train yourself to react constructively rather than defensively to this.

But what none of these listening channels will provide you with is quantified information, and sometimes there is no substitute for that. This is where your listening channels need to be supplemented by formal market research — research that will, for instance, put numbers on an opportunity.

Just as you cannot expect market research to give you the all-important feel for the marketplace, you cannot expect your direct personal contact to give you the quantified data that you need as part of strategic marketing decisions. Market research should be part of your listening system — but like all the other channels, it should be only a part.

I have sketched the kind of listening system we have in our company, one that works for us. But the important point here is not to imitate our listening system, it is to have a formal listening system of some kind. The exact form it takes should reflect the special nature of your business.

You should aim to connect with your customers on the issues that are important to them, at the times and in the places where it is convenient for them to do so.

Arriving at the right system is not something that will happen overnight — indeed, if my experience is any guide, you will be constantly refining and extending your listening system in the light of experience.

Right now, the vital thing is to make a start on building your system.

To sum up the lesson of this chapter: listening to customers is the key to getting a feel for the marketplace, and the first big secret of listening is to put in a listening system — and to work it.

It's a major step towards getting your customers to keep coming back to you.

Chapter 5

*Listening to customers:
the second big secret*

ONE OF THE SIGNS OF A GOOD MANAGER is
an ability to delegate.

It doesn't come naturally to those who are doers, as
most people with a marketing instinct are. It's
something that has to be learned.

What we also have to learn is that there are some
things that just can't be delegated, some things that
managers have to go on doing no matter how high up
the ladder they climb.

Listening to customers is one of those things. So the
second big secret of listening to customers is:

Listen from the top

In a truly customer-driven organization, everybody
listens. But that's not the way it usually is. In the
typical organization, the higher up you go the less
direct listening to customers there is.

Some top people regard listening to customers as
something that their subordinates do, and then report
back to them about.

Wrong !

You are not listening to customers at all if someone
else does your listening for you.

Listening second-hand means that your information
is filtered through other people. That can work with

hard data, but where it won't work is with the feel of the marketplace.

"Feel" is not something you can get second-hand.

This is the real test of the customer-driven leader. Are you prepared to invest the time in getting to know your customers well, and to go on investing that time — year in and year out?

Given that time is the most precious resource available to a top executive, this is asking a lot.

But there is no way around it.

I had to face up to this in 1980 when we were in the middle of getting our large Blackrock Centre off the ground. It was a very big investment for us, millions of dollars.

One day my then secretary, Patricia Keaveney, said to me:

"Can I make an appointment with the architect for Friday afternoon? It's the only time free all week, what with meetings with the lawyer, the builder, the accountant, the bankers, and so on."

I suddenly realized that I was not going to get *near* the shop floor in the coming week.

So I went to a friend whose ability I respected — Vincent O'Doherty — and asked him to join our company as chairman. I wanted him to look after matters such as the multi-million dollar shopping centers, so that I could concentrate on the customer.

When I look back on this decision, which has worked very well, I think I had recognized that getting customers' first-hand opinions about the quality of our tomatoes was as critical to the future of our business as the building of the shopping center.

Today, apart from the time I devote to customer panels, I spend about half my time every week on the floor of our shops, meeting customers.

Many chief executives would consider this a waste of their time, but I don't. I never come away from the shop floor without having learned *something new.*

One of my favorite chores is helping to pack the customers' bags at the checkouts.

Menial? Not at all!

It is an excellent place to meet customers, and the fact that I have something to do as I talk to them means that conversations are more relaxed and natural.

Some top executives subscribe to what I call the "Royal Tour Syndrome." But that's not the way to meet customers.

Customers are not troops to be reviewed; they are people to be *served.* The best way to meet customers is to roll up your sleeves and do the job.

Your public relations people will love it if you do, and this is where you need to be careful.

The PR spin-off from the top man rolling up his sleeves can be valuable, but it's important to remember that it is not an end in itself. In fact, publicity for this kind of thing can be counter-productive — if people think that that is the *only* reason why you do it.

So look into your motives carefully.

In the early days of our company, I had little difficulty finding time to meet customers. I remember when we had four shops, I used to spend a day in each shop, and the fifth day at head office.

But as the company grew, so did the demands on my time. I started the customer panels as a way of keeping in touch with customers, when I was forced to spend less time on the shop floor.

But even with tools like customer panels, keeping in touch *is* time-consuming.

To make sure that it happens, you have to be *convinced* that it is worthwhile.

You have to be *convinced* that a top executive needs this contact, and that he or she can't do the job properly without it.

The catch is that the only way you will convince yourself of this is by doing it!

Keeping in touch with customers is not just a matter for the chief executive. It is a problem for every manager because the very nature of the management function tends to take you away from direct, day-to-day contact with the customers.

It is especially vital for the top management in every company, the people on the chief executive's team — especially those whose functions would normally keep them far away from customer contact.

We have a rule that all our top management must spend half a day each week in the shops, serving the customers in some way.

It's a rule that is very difficult to stick to, but we keep working at it. If there is one thing more difficult for a chief executive than getting himself out of the office and out to where the customers are, it is getting his top management people to do the same!

Mind you, the fact that I don't always succeed with my colleagues gives me an edge: in our management discussions, I am often the one who is best-informed about the marketplace!

Let me give you a trivial example of the difference in perspective between the management suite and the reality of customer contact.

At one stage we had a problem with bottle deposits. The problem arose because, in a typical shop, we might sell 500 dozen returnable bottles a week but customers were bringing us back a lot more — perhaps as many as 700 dozen.

There was a certain irony about this, since it was a problem that we had created for ourselves through our attitude to customer service.

We went to a lot of trouble to make the process of returning the bottles and getting the deposits as easy as possible for the customer. As a result, they preferred to bring back all their bottles to us not just the ones they had bought from us.

Because of the high cost of handling the returned bottles, it was a problem that nagged at us. We burned a lot of "Monday-morning oil" on it, at our weekly management meetings.

Finally, we decided that we had no option but to restrict the returns we accepted to bottles that have been bought from us. We reckoned that this could be explained without much difficulty to customers, and that they would accept it as reasonable.

And we were right.

However, a few days after the change in policy went into effect, one of our managers, Brian Webb, happened to come up to the place in the shop where the returns were being taken in. He paused for a moment, watching as the girl sorted the bottles of one customer.

After a few moments, she found a "foreign" bottle. She said to the customer:

"I'm sorry, that's not one of ours. You'll have to take it back to Dunnes."

At that moment, a bell rang in the manager's head. He suddenly realized just what it was we were doing with this new policy.

We were systematically telling our customers to go to a competitor!

It was one thing to accept that customers sometimes shopped elsewhere, that was a fact of life. It was quite another to give them a *reason* for going back there. And that, unwittingly, was what we had started to do.

Brian told me about his reaction, and I knew immediately that he was right. We knew then that we had to find another way of dealing with our problem.

My point is that what looks logical and acceptable and right in the rarified atmosphere of a management office may not necessarily look the same where it has to be put into effect.

That is why there is no way around it: managers must have constant, real-life contact with the customers. Only then can they make the right decisions.

When I became chairman of the Irish postal service, I put this principle into effect. Even though I was a part-time non-executive chairman, I still thought it worthwhile to spend a day a month actually doing the various jobs that are involved in delivering the mail and serving the public.

Mind you, I found at the beginning that while I had no difficulty relating to the customers, *I did have* some difficulty in getting my cash to balance at the end of a session on a post office counter.

One of the old hands told me that this was often the way: the outgoing people made mistakes, while the person who kept his head down and hardly looked at the customer was the one who never made mistakes with the cash.

This took me aback, because I had found in our business that you could do the two things — be friendly and helpful to customers *and* get the cash right.

Obviously I hadn't understood the difficulty of doing this and that lesson cost me $2.20 which I had to reimburse to the post office!

As in our own company, I found that the top management in the postal service were less than thrilled about the idea of putting in time at the bottom step themselves. Very often their attitude was:

"Yes, you need to do this, because you're new to the postal service. But we don't. We know it all, we did that 20 years ago as we worked our way up the organization. We don't need to go back."

They were wrong, and many people make the same mistake.

The fact is that your marketplace is changing all the time, and to be in touch with it you must go on meeting customers — until the day when you finally hang up your boots and leave the organization for good.

Otherwise, you are taking management decisions based on the past — on a world that may have changed out of all recognition.

One of the most important things that keeping in touch with customers gives you is a sensitivity to change.

Seeing change coming, and adapting quickly to it, is the key to success in any competitive marketplace.

You cannot see that change coming if all your experience of the marketplace is in the past.

So the lesson of this chapter is: no matter what your past experience, the nearer you are to the top of your organization the more vital it is to listen directly to customers.

CHAPTER 6

Listening to customers: the third big secret

YOU HAVE PUT IN A SYSTEM for listening to customers, and that system includes listening from the top.

Is this enough? Not quite. There is a third big secret to put into effect. It has to do with what you listen for.

Think about it: why are you listening at all?

To get a feel for the marketplace.

Yes, certainly — but why?

So that you can serve the marketplace better, so that you can see change coming, so that you can perform better than your competitors.

With these aims, any old listening won't do. **You have to *focus* your listening on what you want to achieve.**

If you don't focus, you will be swamped with material that will be of no use in making you customer driven.

Consider what I call "The Head Waiter Syndrome." We have all experienced this. The head waiter sweeps around the tables in the restaurant, interrogating the diners.

"Everything all right, sir, madam? Enjoying your meal?"

The questions are phrased in such a way as to

assume that the answer will be "yes." The tone of voice, the body language suggest he is only pausing for a moment.

Small wonder that most people docilely give head waiters the answer that they expect.

Is this dialogue? Is this listening to the customer? Of course it isn't!

It succeeds in suppressing all but the strongest criticisms. It does so not least because the customers do not actually believe that the head waiter really wants to know; they perceive the question as a meaningless ritual.

If you invest time in listening to customers but perform your own version of the head-waiter syndrome, then you are totally wasting your time.

Worse than that: you are probably also misleading yourself that things are better than they are. Your listening, instead of giving you a feel for the marketplace, has given you a bum steer.

So remember: time spent on listening does not automatically produce a dividend. It may even be counter-productive.

Does that put you off the whole idea of investing in listening to customers? If, after all, you can't be sure that it pays off, why bother?

Relax!

There is a very simple way to ensure that listening to your customers is productive. You do it by applying the third big secret of listening to customers:

Make sure to hear what you don't want to hear.

What don't you want to hear?

Make a list of the things you would rather not hear from customers.

For instance, you don't want to hear:

- that they think your prices are too high;
- that they don't like your pet new product or service;
- that they feel the quality of your product or service is deteriorating;
- that they are tired of buying your product or service, or that they feel it no longer meets their needs,
- that they think your competitors are better than you in any way; that they are thinking of transferring their business somewhere else.

You would much prefer not to hear any of that. In fact, let's be absolutely honest about it: all you really want to hear is *applause!*

You want to go out into the marketplace and hear a chorus of:

"We love it! We love you! Give us more!"

Now here's the funny thing. You are, in fact, more likely to hear praise than blame.

This is so for two reasons: first, because in general customers do tend to praise more than to blame. And second, because the sound of the praise drowns out the sound of the blame. You hear selectively, and what sticks with you is the praise.

This is where the need to focus comes in. You have to face the fact that listening to customers praise you has very little value in making you customer-driven.

I am not saying it has no value at all — it can be important in reinforcing your determination, and both you and your staff would not be human if they did not react to praise as a stimulant to further effort.

But the *real* value in listening to customers comes from discovering what they don't like, what hasn't worked, what needs to be changed, what the other guy is doing better. The real value is in hearing all the things you *don't* want to hear.

It can sometimes be remarkably difficult to elicit these reactions. I remember well our very first customer panels. They seemed like a good idea in theory, but at the first sessions all we got was *praise.*

It was as if the customers had come along specifically to tell us how good we were. Everything was great, everything was lovely, keep it up!

The difficulty was that people were just not in the habit of offering constructive criticism, unless they had a very specific problem fresh in their mind and still annoying them.

There was also the problem, in those early days, that people did not really believe we wanted to hear criticism. Quite apart from the fact that they felt that offering criticism was letting down the staff in the shop whom they knew and liked.

We persisted in trying to elicit criticism, and eventually succeeded. Finally, some customer would respond to the suggestion, "But there must be some way you think we could do things better?"

And once the first, tentative criticism had been voiced, the floodgates would open. Other customers would join in, and we would — at last! — be launched into the real world.

My point is that this is a stage you have to go through, a barrier you have to surmount. If you don't, you will be carrying out your own version of the head-waiter syndrome. And you will be totally wasting the time you spend talking to customers.

When you exercise to lose weight or keep fit, you're told that it isn't doing you any good until you start sweating. When listening to customers, it isn't doing you any good until you start hearing the criticism, until you start hearing the things you don't want to hear.

A final word about listening, before we move on to the practicalities of one particular way of doing it — customer panels.

Don't expect your customers to do the whole job for you.

Often they will — they will make useful practical suggestions; they will come up with a simple solution for a problem that you thought was impossible to solve.

But a lot of the time they will leave you with a lot of work to do as well.

An example that springs to my mind in our own case concerns sausages.

Occasionally we got comments that amounted to mild dissatisfaction with the sausages we sold. Customers sometimes complained about their lack of freshness, about their price, about the fact that we didn't stock a particular sausage that they liked.

At one stage we decided to take all these comments on board and attack the sausage problem once and for all. So we gave all those comments to one particular manager, and said to him:

"Create the best sausage department in Dublin. Here's what the customers think is wrong with the way we do things. You find out how to do it right, and when we know we've got it right, the other shops can copy it."

He went off and did what we asked.

He bought new refrigerators to hold the sausages — the latest type.

He took on more lines, so that his shop offered a far wider range than before — and a wider range than anyone else.

He attacked the freshness problem by deciding that there would be new stock every day — we would never sell yesterday's sausages. This involved doing a special deal to ensure daily deliveries from the suppliers, and also making sure that the day's stock was cleared every night.

He did all this, and the deal also included lower prices than ever before. He then started to listen to what his customers thought about the changes.

After a while, he came to me and said:

"They're still not satisfied. They're still not happy with our sausages."

Now here was a real problem. We had done everything they had suggested, and it wasn't working.

We didn't know what was lacking. Neither did the customers, so far as we could find out. But something was missing!

Some time after that an American friend of mine,

Michael O'Connor, discovered that it was possible to make sausages on a very small scale — he saw it being done in a German supermarket. The idea appealed to me, and we put a "sausage kitchen" into one of our shops.

In it we made the sausages on the spot, right in front of the customers.

Bingo!

We discovered that this was what had been lacking, the element that customers felt was missing but were not able to identify.

What they really wanted was a kind of sausage service that no longer existed. Their vague feelings of dissatisfaction were against the whole idea of "factory" sausages.

When we offered them sausages that were "homemade," produced before their eyes, they no longer had any doubts about their freshness or their wholesomeness.

And by listening carefully to their reactions, we were able to produce sausages exactly to their taste — fine-tuning our recipes again and again.

Within a very short time our sausages became famous, and from being a problem, sausages soon became one of our selling points. And, I may add, a very satisfactory source of profit as well.

But my point is that very often listening to customers is only *the first step* on the way to finding a solution for the problem that you hear.

Crowning the Customer

CHAPTER 7

How to make customer panels work

ONE GOOD PLACE TO START CREATING your system for listening to customers might well be with the concept of customer panels. This is so for at least two reasons:

First, customer panels are a *visible* demonstration of listening commitment.

A decision to set up customer panels is a signal, both inside and outside your organization, that you are taking listening seriously. But I don't mean this only from a public relations point of view, important though that may be. A decision to set up customer panels is hard to go back on, once made — to do so would involve a loss of face. So they are an excellent tool to stiffen your resolve.

Second, customer panels immediately provide a lot of material which can be easily recirculated throughout your organization. They therefore offer a very quick way of getting results in your campaign to become customer-driven.

I am now going to give a few hints about how to run customer panels effectively, but I confess that I do so with a certain amount of trepidation. When I set up our own customer panels back in 1975, I did so without the benefit of any guidance from anyone else. I made some mistakes, and learned what I believed were (and still are) good lessons.

However, a few years after we got up and running I came across a set of guidelines for customer panels issued by the Food Marketing Institute in the US. On several key points, they directly contradicted our own experience! So the best approach may well be to try for yourself rather than take any advice.

So with that caveat, here are my tips:

1. In selecting your panel, touch all the bases but don't worry too much about being fully representative

It's certainly important that your customer panels include people drawn from as many of the different segments of your customer base as possible. But while your group should be diverse, it need not reflect precisely the composition of your market in the same way that a market research sample should.

Concentrate your energy on seeing that all the bases are touched, rather than in filling quotas for each type of customer. What you are after is a diversity of views, not a statistical representation of the strength of each view. (Customer panels are not the tool to give you that kind of data.)

2. Don't pay your panel members

I have found that the most useful participants in a customer panel are people who are interested enough to give up some of their time to come along. People who have to be "bribed" to come along are much more likely to tell you what they think you want to hear. People who are doing you a favor by coming are much less likely to feel under an obligation to you, and are therefore more likely to be trenchant in their views.

We usually send our panel members a little token at Christmas, but it is not part of the deal. By the time they receive it from us, they know very well that what we value is their outspokenness.

3. Let your customers set the agenda

There is a big temptation to structure the business of a customer panel according to your own expectations. You know what is important for you to find out, therefore you set an agenda to reflect that.

Wrong!

One of the most important things you may learn from a customer panel is what the customers' priorities are. They will tell you, if you let them. But by structuring the agenda too rigidly, you can make it impossible for them to do that. You may also make it impossible for them to comment on issues that are important to them, because they don't see an obvious place for it on your agenda.

In running our customer panels, I do no more than make sure that the entire shopping experience is covered in the course of the meeting. From time to time I may have specific questions that I ask along the way. But the overall principle is that our customers set the agenda, not us.

4. Keep your side as small as possible

You need someone from your company to run the meeting, and someone to take notes. In our company, I always run the meetings and the notes are taken by a customer relations specialist. That's all: we are two, and the customers can number up to 12 or 14.

I believe it is important to be heavily outnumbered in meetings like this. The smaller the company representation, the more the customers will feel that it is their show and the more likely they will be to speak their mind and make constructive contributions.

5. Be aware of the flattery obstacle

When we first started customer panels, we had great difficulty getting our customers to say anything uncomplimentary about us at all!

There are several reasons why people can be reluctant to criticize. One is that they may be reluctant to get staff into trouble. For instance, when we started off I used to run the customer panels with the local manager at my side. The customers would not utter a word of criticism, because they didn't want to let down "their" manager in front of his boss!

For this reason, I took to holding the panels on my own without the manager present. I then had to work very hard to convince the customers that my only wish was to improve their shopping experience, not to make trouble for anyone in the shop. One of the ways I did this was by persuading them that any shortcomings they encountered were my fault, not anybody else's.

I sometimes arrive purposely five minutes late for the meeting. This allows Margaret Jones, the person who takes notes for me at the panel and who is a shopper herself, to open up with *her* current pet grouse in my absence. This helps to make the customers understand our willingness to hear criticism, so that by the time I arrive they are all ready to jump on me!

6. Don't answer back

When you do succeed in eliciting criticism, one of the biggest temptations is to spend a large part of the available time answering the criticism.

This is a very natural response — an instinctive one. It is, however, one you must train yourself to resist. If you don't do so, the balance of the customer panel will soon shift. Before you know what is happening, the customers will perceive the occasion as being company-driven rather than customer-driven. And if that happens, the flow of useful comments, suggestions and criticisms will dry up.

I have always found it useful, in fighting the temptation to respond immediately to criticism, to remember how small the group is. If we have a dozen members in a group, at a shop that has 20,000 regular customers, then in a sense each panel member represents more than 1,500 people. I can reach that individual panel member to answer the criticism, but how about the other 1,500 people? I can never rule out the possibility that the people who are not there at the panel have the same criticism as the person now talking.

This attitude helps me to remember the right way to respond to criticism at a customer panel: to continue to probe, for more and more information — both from the customer who raised the issue and from the others present.

Very often, that probing uncovers new suggestions for dealing with the problem. At worst, it leaves me much better informed as to the exact nature of the customer response — and therefore much better equipped to deal with it.

7. Circulate a report on each customer panel widely within your organization

The person who will benefit most, by far, from your customer panel is the person who runs it. Nothing beats face-to-face contact with customers.

However, there is a wealth of value to be gained from circulating and discussing a report on the panel meeting. You should aim to circulate it as widely as possible. I have found that doing so gives a clear and regular reminder to everyone in the organization that we are *really* interested in what our customers think.

In our own company, the panel report is circulated first of all to the top management team, who discuss it at their weekly management meeting. In addition, it goes to all the branch managers and to executives in a wide variety of functions throughout the organization.

Within each shop it is circulated by the manager to

the different departments. As a matter of routine, the report is also circulated by Anne OBroin, my personal assistant, to people outside the organization — our advertising agency, public relations consultants, and so on — who could benefit from this regular insight into what our customers are thinking.

Writing the report is something that needs to be done with care. For instance, I always say at the beginning of each meeting:

"Don't worry about naming any of our people. If it's a compliment, we'll leave the name in; if it's a complaint, we'll omit the name."

So the report will read:

"There is a man on the fish counter who is quite rude," and "Jean on the deli is very helpful."

We also recognize the danger of "editorializing," and therefore try to present the report as much as possible in the form of direct quotes from customers' comments made at the meeting. An advantage of the direct quote approach is that it reduces the temptation to turn individual comments into generalizations about the marketplace.

Another advantage of the direct quote is that very often it catches precisely the strength and depth of feeling that lies behind a customer's criticism.

8. Take action on the comments, suggestions and criticisms

Follow-up of customer panels is vital. It is important from the viewpoint of the participating customers: unless they feel that their contribution is actually getting results, the quality of their input will fall off very quickly.

But follow-up is also vital to keep the momentum going within the company for the customer panel idea. To justify the time and effort that regular customer panels demand, it is important that concrete results are seen to flow from them. So do not use them just to get a feel for the marketplace — use them also as the basis for making decisions.

This does not mean that you must implement every idea that emerges from a customer panel. Not all of them will be practical, or economic. But as with everything else in the customer-driven approach, you should take the attitude "Why not?" to the suggestions that emerge, instead of concentrating your energy on rejecting them.

With a positive approach, you will be amazed how often it is possible to implement the ideas that customers give you. And the first time you make money from a customer's idea, you will become a real convert to this virtually untapped source of profit.

The lesson of this chapter is that customer panels are probably the single most important element you can use in a listening system, provided you use them in the right way.

Chapter 8

How (and why) to create more complaints

PEOPLE USUALLY THINK THAT customer complaints are a bad thing.

If your aim is to keep your customers coming back for more, then your aim should be to run a business where there will be no customer complaints at all. And if that's so, any complaint is a sign of failure. The fewer complaints you have, the better.

Right?

Wrong!

Certainly your aim should be to achieve perfection. But no matter how good you are, you will never quite reach it. There will *always* be some failures, always some room for complaint.

And if you really want to achieve perfection, it is in your interest to uncover those complaints and to learn from them.

What people seldom realize is that there are two factors that affect the number of complaints you get.

One factor is the number of things you do wrong.

The other, often forgotten, factor is your customers' expectation of how you will deal with the complaint.

A customer once said to me:

"Of course we complain to you, because we know you'll take it seriously. We wouldn't bother complaining to [one of our competitors] —they'd just give us a hard time. It's not worth the hassle."

This illustrates the fact that there is one very easy way to reduce the number of complaints, if that is what you want to do:

Just handle the complaints very badly.

Very soon the message will get around, and the number of complaints will fall off dramatically.

Unfortunately, many companies — perhaps most — need no lessons in how to handle complaints *badly*.

They make it difficult for customers to complain. They handle complaints grudgingly. Above all, they show a lack of trust in their customers.

All too often, their customers end up feeling that *they* are in the wrong, not the company they are complaining to.

This is commercial suicide!

By taking that attitude to complaints, you are giving your customers a very good reason for not coming back to you. The very opposite to what you should be trying to achieve, if your aim is to be customer driven.

And yet, companies who are driving their complainers away often congratulate themselves on the low level of complaints that they get.

Some companies even measure their service performance by the number of complaints they receive, hailing any reduction in the figure as a sign of progress.

The truth is that a reduction in the number of complaints does not necessarily mean a reduction in the number of customer problems.

If you reduce the number of complaints without

reducing the number of problems, then in the long run what you are doing is reducing the number of your *customers.*

There are two reasons why it is in your interest to uncover every customer problem, and encourage every customer with a problem to make a complaint about it.

The first reason is that, although a customer problem represents a failure by your company, it is also a golden opportunity not just to recover the lost ground but to actually *improve* your relationship with the customer as well.

We're slow to admit this because we have a faulty mental model of how customers' minds work.

What we *think* happens is something like this:

1. Before the problem: Customer satisfied
2. Problem arises: Customer less satisfied
3. Complaint handled well: Customer satisfied

In other words, the conventional model suggests that handling a complaint well succeeds in restoring customer satisfaction back to where it was before the problem arose.

In my experience, this is not the way it works at all.
The real model is:

1. Before the problem: Customer satisfied
2. Problem arises: Customer less satisfied.
3. Complaint handled well: Customer more satisfied than before

Handling a complaint well is like making a touchdown. It can deepen your relationship with that customer, and make him or her more likely to come back to you to do more business.

But in terms of the benefits that good complaint handling can bring you, this is only the tip of the iceberg.

The *real* pay-off is much greater.

In chapter 4, I called complaints the safety-valve of any business. That's true. They are an invaluable early-warning system.

Their value arises from this fact of business life:

The complaints that you get are only a sample of the problems that exist.

There is a temptation to regard each complaint as an exception. Even if it were an exception, it would still be worth your while dealing with it properly. But in fact the complaint you see is almost always representative of many that you don't.

How many?

A dozen?

A hundred?

We don't know.

And that lack of knowledge should keep you awake at night.

It should worry you because of what happens when customers have a problem that they *don't* complain about.

Almost always, they talk about it — to other people, to other customers or potential customers.

Most people do not complain — they grumble. A grumble, in my book, is *a complaint to the wrong person.* Instead of making a complaint to the people who were responsible for the problem, they sound off to those who were not.

It's your task to turn grumbles into complaints. And if you need an incentive to do this, let me throw some mathematics at you.

I saw some research recently that showed this: dissatisfied customers are 20 times more likely to talk about their experiences to other people than satisfied customers are.

If that's true, it should bring home to you just how dangerous dissatisfied customers can be.

Suppose, for instance, you have 95 percent satisfied customers and 5 percent dissatisfied ones. You might be tempted to think that that was a pretty good situation.

Maybe.

But not if what is happening is this:

5 dissatisfied custo-mers each telling 20 other people about their bad experience	=	100 people hearing **bad** news about you
95 satisfied customers each telling 1 other person about their good experience	=	95 people hearing **good** news about you

So even with 95 percent satisfied customers, you can still be losing out on the vital word-of-mouth publicity that every business needs!

Obviously, it is in your interest to reduce the number of your dissatisfied customers to the absolute minimum. And handling complaints properly offers you an opportunity of doing that.

If you can once get the person to complain, you have a chance of sending them away satisfied rather than dissatisfied (in fact, as I have said, possibly more satisfied than before).

So your aim should be to get the number of customer complaints to *equal* the number of customer problems. That way, there would be no unresolved problems out there festering, and creating dissatisfied customers.

You do *not*, of course, have an interest in having things go wrong in your company. There is a trap here to beware of.

When people in business come to realize how much mileage they can make from handling complaints well, they sometimes become less anxious to avoid complaints in the first place.

"Well, sure if anything goes wrong we can cope with it— and maybe even come out better in the end."

No!

That is not the way to become customer-driven. That is not the way to keep your customers coming back. For one thing, it forgets the majority of customers who do *not* complain when they have a problem.

So your quality control should always aim to reduce to the minimum the number of causes for complaint that you create.

But your service attitude should be to ensure that

whenever there *is* a cause for complaint, that it does turn into a complaint — and not into a dissatisfied customer.

Already we have gained two big benefits from handling complaints properly: we can increase customer satisfaction among those who do complain, and we can reduce the damage that is created by problems that do not get complained about.

But there is, of course, a further benefit.

Every complaint gives us the opportunity to improve what we offer customers.

Dealing properly with a complaint is not just a matter of keeping that particular customer satisfied. Much more important, it is a matter of learning from the mistake. Every time a complaint is made, part of the process of dealing with it should be to ask: can we stop this problem from arising again?

Looked at this way, your complaints procedure can be part of an overall company improvement program. It can turn complaints from being a cost burden into a profit opportunity.

So much for the benefits. How can you handle complaints properly? In fact, given that it is so important, the right things to do are remarkably simple:

1. Express regret quickly

If a customer has a problem, any problem, that is or should be — a matter of genuine regret for you. You can help the process along by expressing that regret at the very outset.

Remember that you can do this without admitting
any liability (which may be important from a legal
point of view in some cases). Do not use the liability
issue as an excuse to avoid saying that you are sorry
the customer has had a problem in dealing with you.

2. Trust the customer

A tiny proportion of customers are dishonest and
will try to take advantage of a complaints procedure.
Because of this, some companies approach all complaints with suspicion — and so alienate the vast
majority of customers who are perfectly honest.

Look at your procedures: do they assume guilt or
innocence on the part of the customer? Are you
expecting the customer to prove the truth of what
they are saying, as in a court of law? Or does your
procedure assume that the customer is telling the
truth?

In my experience, it is possible to build in
safeguards to a complaints procedure that prevent it
from being abused — without creating the
atmosphere of distrust that very often puts people
right off complaining.

3. Never, never put the customer in the wrong

"The customer is always right" is a time-honored
cliche. What I find more useful as a guiding maxim is
the notion that you must never put the customer in
the wrong. There is no way you can win by doing so;
on the contrary, it is a sure way to lose the customer.

Let me tell you when I first learned this lesson.

Shortly after we opened our first Dublin shop, I encountered a customer one Saturday afternoon. She was heading for the butcher's counter, and she was almost in tears.

"I bought this rib steak from you an hour ago, and when I got it home I discovered there was a terrible smell off it."

I whisked her over to the butcher's counter, where the head butcher, Jim McGrath, listened sympathetically and then said:

"It's awful that you had to come back. Hold on a minute, and I'll take it outside in the fresh air and give it a smell."

I went outside with him and we both smelled the meat carefully. Neither of us could get any smell.

Jim went back into the shop, and said to the customer:

"Look, how about I give you a nice bit of sirloin instead? That will maybe make up for the trouble you had in coming back."

The customer was pleased by that, and as she was waiting for him to cut the meat she said to me:

"Oh, I'm very relieved you got a smell. My husband said it was the glue from the model airplane that my son was putting together in the kitchen when I brought the shopping in."

"Well, actually we didn't smell anything," I said. "But it's no problem to give you the sirloin instead."

At that, the woman burst into tears and rushed out of the shop. As I looked after her in dismay, Jim came up behind me.

101

"What happened?" he asked.

I told him what I had said, in my innocence.

He swore at me — and I'm the boss!

"Aren't you the right one? Why did you have to tell her that she was wrong? *Never* do that! I promise you, we'll never see that woman again."

And we did not.

But I learned my lesson.

Customers may not always be right. But there is never any percentage for you in telling them that they are wrong.

They will, literally, never forgive you for doing that.

4. Don't pass the buck — accept responsibility

Very often, your customer will have a problem that has been caused by someone else. This happens to us a lot in retailing, where we sell other people's products.

However, we accept that the customer's problem is always our problem: we don't pass the customer on to someone else, we make sure that we ourselves leave the customer satisfied.

(Of course, this doesn't mean that we don't take up the complaint with our supplier. We certainly do, as part of our effort to avoid a recurrence of the problem.)

Remember nothing annoys customers more than being passed on from Frank to Jack. Try to ensure that the customer only has to complain once: every time they have to tell their story, their grievance is likely to grow.

There is a further variation on this principle. I believe that you should try to get involved in solving a customer's problem, even when neither you nor one of your suppliers is responsible for having caused it.

Sometimes problems arise that are really nobody's fault. You shouldn't try to duck them because of that. The fact that a customer has a problem is enough reason to accept responsibility for trying to solve it.

Here's an example. One day — it was coming up to Christmas — a customer came into one of our shops. She was very upset indeed about something that had happened to her 16-year-old daughter, who had been shopping the previous day.

The girl had left her gloves behind her at the checkout. A few seconds later, the checkout girl saw the gloves and immediately called over the nearest other member of staff — who happened to be the security man stationed at the door.

"Would you run after that girl in the blue coat?" she said. "I think she's left these gloves behind."

The security man went straight out into the street and spotted her before she disappeared out of sight.

He went up to her and said: "Excuse me, did you leave your gloves behind in Superquinn?"

The girl looked down at her hands. "Oh, yes! I must have."

"Not to worry. We have them inside for you."

And the two of them walked back to the shop, where she picked up the gloves from the checkout and went off happy.

End of another "customer service" story? Not quite. This one turned out badly.

The following day, two different neighbors of the girl's family came up to her mother and said:

"Oh, I see your girl was in trouble yesterday. I saw her being brought into Superquinn by the security man."

Seeing her walking back to the shop with the security man, the neighbors had jumped to the conclusion that she was being apprehended for shoplifting. No wonder the woman was upset!

"My daughter's name is ruined!"

Here was a problem that wasn't our *fault*, in the usual sense. It had happened because we were trying to be helpful. There was no question of our being legally liable in any way. And yet, it was our problem — because it was our customer's problem. So I immediately decided to help to put things right.

But what were we to do?

This certainly wasn't a problem that money could solve. The problem was: how to undo the damage?

In the end, what we came up with was this. As it was near Christmas, we decided to give the girl a temporary job for two weekends during her school holidays.

We put her working on the customer service desk, where everybody would see her and would immediately realize that she was *persona grata* with us.

We even went one step further: we arranged for a photograph to go into a local paper, showing her as one of a group of staff making preparations in the shop for Christmas. I am glad to say that it worked.

The point is: if your customer has a problem, no matter what it is, you have a problem.

5. Try to settle the complaint quickly

Think of a complaint as a festering wound: until it is resolved, it gets worse. And until it is resolved, your customer is far more likely to be talking about it to other people.

Look at your procedures and see how much time elapses between the time a customer complains and the matter is resolved. Aim to reduce that time to the minimum.

Sometimes when a customer complains, you will need to do your own checking before you can respond fully — and this may take some time. If this cannot be avoided, respond *immediately* with an expression of regret that the customer had the problem and explain the procedure you are going through.

6. Above all, make it known that you welcome complaints

In the long run, the most effective way to advertise the fact that you welcome complaints is by the way that you handle them — word will soon get around.

But when installing a new system for handling complaints, you do need to go out and sell it to your customers. Through notices, advertising, direct mail, or whatever medium is appropriate, make it clear that you welcome complaints as a way of improving your service.

You also need to sell it to your staff, so that they see

complaints as a service opportunity and not as a criticism of themselves to which they react defensively. There is no point in telling your customers that you welcome complaints if they experience the exact opposite when they do actually complain.

7. And finally, make sure to thank your customers for complaining

If you develop the right attitude to complaints, you will genuinely become very grateful to the customers who do complain. Express that gratitude, and explain to them why you take complaints so seriously.

If you ever find difficulty in feeling grateful to a customer who complains, consider this. A little while ago, an American colleague of mine was coming to Dublin from Norway via London.

At London he missed the flight because it was not announced over the public-address system. Through close questioning of the airline staff, he discovered that the flight had been overbooked and they had deliberately not announced the flight in the hope of eliminating one or two passengers and therefore having less of a problem to cope with.

He was, quite rightly, incensed. And when he eventually arrived in Dublin one of his first actions was to change his return bookings to another airline.

I told him that he should write a letter of complaint to the airline's chief executive.

"No!" he said. "I don't want to help those crooks. They screwed me up, and I'm damned if I'm going to help them in any way."

So when a person does complain, be grateful. The alternative could have hurt you a lot more.

The lesson of this chapter is that you can make complaints into a positive thing for your company and you *should* do so.

Chapter 9

*How to see customers
as people*

NO MATTER WHO YOU SELL TO, your
customers are *people*.

Even if you sell your product or service to giant
companies or to governments, it is people — not
organizations or machines — who make the buying
decisions and who decide whether or not to come
back to do more business with you.

But for some reason, it seems to be very easy to
forget that customers are people — even if you are in
a business that deals face-to-face with people all the
time.

It is very easy to fall into the trap of looking at
customers impersonally, of treating them as if they
were pieces of machinery on an assembly-line.

**Almost every shopper has had the experience of
being treated as if they did not exist.**

In the supermarket business, the classic example is
the two checkout operators who talk to each other
animatedly as they check out the goods, totally
ignoring the customers standing beside them.

Perhaps it is the numbers that do it. We have no
difficulty in relating one-to-one to our relatives or
friends; but when we meet people in large numbers
there is a temptation to regard them as elements of
that big crowd rather than as individuals.

If you or your staff look on your customers merely as numbers, then you will be tempted to deal with them as quickly as possible rather than as well as possible.

I have always been fascinated by the obvious pleasure that some shop assistants get from telling a customer that they don't have what the customer wants. For some reason you find this very often in bookshops.

"No, we don't have it! Why don't you try across the road?" (That being the competitor.)

I think it arises because *some people see customers as just so many problems to be disposed of.* The sooner each one can be disposed of, the better. So since the quickest possible way to dispose of a customer is to say "no", there is perhaps some satisfaction in being able to end the matter so quickly.

Whatever the reason, this kind of thing becomes the refusal to see and treat customers as people.

And it is something that you must conquer if you are to become truly customer-driven. Because it is human interaction that supplies the spark to customer relationships and sets them alight.

Over the years, I have developed a number of techniques that I use myself and have passed on to our staff — techniques that are aimed at creating this all-important personal relationship between our company and its customers.

Let's begin with the absolute basics. Was it Dale Carnegie who said: "The sweetest sound in the whole world is the sound of your own name"? Whoever said it was perfectly right. Nothing helps to establish rapport with a customer more effectively than using their name.

Why?

Because, of course, the person's name is what identifies them as an individual: it is unique to them.

In using their name, we are treating them straight away as an individual — not a statistic, or a number, or a member of an anonymous class like "passengers" or "customers."

- **Using a person's name never fails to establish personal rapport.**

It never fails because the act itself carries its own guarantee of sincerity.

If a person uses my name, it means that they have taken a certain amount of trouble to do so. I don't have to believe that they really care about me, or that they will remember my name tomorrow to be impressed — all I have to acknowledge is that they took a certain minimum amount of trouble to find out who I was and to use my name.

Take the simplest example. You use your credit card. In returning it, the person serving you can say either:

"Thank you very much, sir. Hope we'll see you again here, soon."

Or:

"Thank you very much, Mr. Quinn. Hope to see you again here, soon."

If said sincerely, the first response is perfectly friendly.

But, by comparison, the second response is MAGIC!

It is magic even when we know that all the person had to do was glance at your name on your credit card and read it off to you.

Even when we are fully aware how minimal the effort was, we are still warmed by the gesture.

This is why in Superquinn we encourage all our staff to go to a considerable amount of trouble to get to know their customers' names, and to use them whenever they can.

For instance, a manager in one of our stores will probably get to know several thousand customers by sight, and eventually will know several hundred by name. That knowledge is worth money in the bank.

From time to time we have set up weeks in our shops when we invite each customer entering the shop to wear a name badge which we provide. The customers always enjoy the occasion, and every time we do it our staff get to know the names of more customers.

But the first rule about using customer names is to take full advantage of the information that you already have.

- When a customer offers a credit card, or a check guarantee card, or a ticket with their name on it, you are being handed information on a plate — use it!
- A restaurant may know your name because you reserved a table, but how often do they use it once you are there?
- A switchboard operator asks for your name before trying to connect you, but then fails to use it

when she comes back a few seconds later to talk to you again.

Remember, too, using a customer's name is particularly effective when you have to say "no." A person who says:

"Mr. Quinn, I'm sorry we're not going to be able to help you. You see . . ." has already reduced the intensity of my disappointment, though I may not realize it.

Nowadays, technology offers us the opportunity to use customers' names more. One of the reasons I enjoy using Sheraton Hotels around the world is because I am impressed with how they have used technology to enhance their customer service.

Does it make a difference, after a long and tiring plane journey, to check into a new hotel for the first time and be greeted by name the first time you pick up the phone to ask for room service? I think it does.

Hotels can do this now because their telephone system can be linked to their reservations computer. As a result, when a customer rings down from his room, the operator's screen instantly displays his name.

A gimmick? No. A worthwhile investment in enhanced customer service. And incidentally, a good example of how technology can be used to extend the reach of people providing service, rather than to replace them with impersonal machinery.

Mind you, you don't always need technology to increase your use of customers' names. A little ingenuity goes a long way. Sometimes, it can even get you into trouble.

I remember a little while ago I was packing bags at the checkout of our branch in Bray, County Wicklow, when a family arrived together at my checkout — a woman, her husband, and her teenage son. Chatting with her as I packed the bags, I casually used her name. They went off and I thought no more about it until a few minutes later when the woman came back into the shop from the parking lot in a distressed state.

It seems her husband had been shattered by the fact that I knew his wife's name! How could I possibly know it, he wondered, when none of them had ever been in the shop before — they lived 60 miles away, and just happened to stop by that shop on their way back from Dublin. His wife said she had never met me before in her life, and yet I knew her name.

Would I please come out to the carpark and convince her husband that we were not having an illicit liaison?

Fortunately, it was easy to do so. I pointed out that I liked to use customers' names wherever possible, and on that occasion I had noticed (because I look for these things) that the teenage son was wearing a scarf with his surname clearly marked on it.

After using names, the most important step towards seeing your customers as people is to actually *look at them*.

It is harder to pretend that a person does not exist if you are looking them in the eye. (This is, of course, why waiters and bartenders get so good at avoiding eye-contact when they are busy. The problem is that many people lose the habit of making eye-contact altogether, with disastrous consequences for customer rapport.)

The eyes are where we make person-to-person contact. I can talk to you without looking at you. That is one-way communication. I can even point out something to you with a gesture of my hand — again I can do this without looking at you, and it is still one-way communication.

But as soon as our eyes lock, we have begun a relationship; with our eyes in contact, we are relating to each other as *people*.

It is very easy to slip out of eye-contact with customers, especially if the job you are doing gives you a reason to do so. If you are chopping up meat as you speak to a customer, you need to look at what you are doing so that you don't chop your fingers off! But you also need to remember to look up from time to time to regain the eye-contact.

One of the techniques we have developed is to encourage staff to make the first approach to a customer: to greet them as they come within range, and not to leave the customer with the responsibility for establishing eye-contact.

Sometimes the people who design technology for customer applications do not realize the importance of eye-contact. For instance, when we began to install scanning checkouts in our shops, we discovered that most of the equipment we were offered positioned the operators so that they and the customers were not directly facing each other.

This was unacceptable to us, because we saw one of

the great benefits of scanning technology as freeing the operator to give more attention to the customer. In the old days of cash-registers, the operator had to sit at 90 degrees to the customer and spend a lot of time with her eyes on the keys and on the price-tags of the products as they were checked. That wasn't necessary any more, but the new technology was not taking advantage of the fact.

We persevered, and eventually we found equipment that met our needs.

You may think that eye-contact is only important when dealing with customers in situations like retailing or catering where large numbers are involved. This is not so. It is important in any business activity. It is, of course, vital in sales presentation — but beyond that, it is equally important in routine contacts with customers.

How much time do people spend in meetings looking at their papers, looking at the table, looking at the floor, looking out of the window — looking almost anywhere but at the people they are in conference with?

If you are in the physical presence of your customer — as opposed to speaking over the phone — you are wasting a large part of your time if you are not maintaining frequent eye-contact.

Here's one more basic in your campaign to see your customers as people: **learn the power of the smile.**

Smiling is another of the great building-blocks of personal relationships. It's something that only people do, after all. Machines don't smile at you, buildings don't smile at you, companies don't smile at you. But people do.

A sincere smile is a signal to the other person that you are ready to relate to them as an individual. It's an offer of friendship that is very difficult to resist.

As a teenager in my father's holiday camp, one of my jobs was as a photographer. We took lots of pictures of the guests, then posted the proofs up on a board where they could see them. They could then order copies of any they liked.

I very rapidly found that people would only buy photographs that showed them smiling — never photographs that showed them with a serious expression.

That was my first introduction to the power of the smile.

In our business now, we attach a lot of importance to smiling. So much so that we use it as a criterion for selecting people in the first place.

I heard once that in the 1930s, one of the big multinational companies used to ruthlessly reject any job candidate who turned up for an interview without a white handkerchief in his breast pocket. Whether it was an effective selection procedure I have no idea, but we have a similar kind of benchmark. As a person walks into the interview, we watch to see how readily they smile.

If they do not smile readily, we take the view that they will probably not be right for our company. Because we are looking for people who are naturally outgoing, and who will enjoy dealing with customers.

But even with a company full of natural smilers, we have to encourage ourselves to actually smile a lot as

117

we work. One of the reasons we tend not to smile is because we are concentrating on what we are doing — whether that is thinking or doing something with our hands. We have to remind ourselves that a frown of concentration is usually seen by the outside world as a frown of unfriendliness or rejection.

A problem that people often raise when I advocate more smiling is the question of sincerity. If we have to work at smiling, are we not being insincere? If we don't feel like smiling, isn't it more honest to let our faces show that, rather than put on a fixed, artificial smile.

I think the truth is that smiling is not only a reflection of how we feel, it also helps to determine how we feel.

If we remember to smile, then the act of smiling at people will tend to put us in a better mood. One of the reasons for this is that if we smile, people will smile back at us — and that helps to cheer us up. On the other hand, if we are gloomy we will get no friendly responses from people and our mood is likely to become gloomier.

Names, eye-contact and smiling — these are three basics. Now here's another technique that is not so basic.

The problem, remember, is the temptation to relate to customers not as individual people but as statistics. Why are we tempted to do that? One of the reasons may be because we know so little about them, if we are dealing with large numbers. Our customers may just be faces in a crowd.

If you have just a small number of customers, it may

be feasible and appropriate for you to actually get to know them better. Then you see a rounded picture of them as human beings, and not just the cardboard figures that add up to their role as customers. If you see them as rounded human beings, then you will find it easier to see things from their point of view and to serve them better because of it.

But if you deal with several thousand customers every week, it is obviously totally impracticable to get to know many of them in any meaningful way. What can you do?

One technique I have found highly useful is to encourage our staff to invent stories about each customer.

We've all done this in restaurants or airport lounges: we look at people and try to invent a scenario that fits in with what we can observe of them. It's a harmless parlor game and a great time-killer, but in business it can have a very useful role.

If you're serving behind a butcher's counter, and you're approached by a face in the crowd, you can invent a story that fills out your picture of the customer.

The customer is asking advice about a particular cut of meat: you can invent a scenario in which she needs that advice because, perhaps, she is entertaining her husband's boss to dinner (or her own boss!) that evening.

Obviously you need to adjust your scenario to fit the information you are given, but the important thing is not to get the scenario right but to jog your mind into relating to the person as an individual.

A variation is this approach is to cast your customer in a role that demands very high standards, perhaps much higher than you think the customer actually demands.

An example I use is to pretend that the approaching customer is Egon Ronay, the international expert on cuisine. Pretend you are serving him, and all of a sudden you have no difficulty in motivating yourself to provide only the highest quality in serving this customer.

These are tricks, but they are not dishonest or tricky. They are simple techniques aimed at jerking your mind out of automatic pilot when you are relating to customers. They help to inhibit you from dealing with people in a one-dimensional way.

There is another thing that you need to be careful about in relating to customers. This is seeing them not as people but as socio-demographic entities. It is one of the bad by-products of market research, and it is a problem experienced by people who are not close enough to the actual flesh-and-blood of the marketplace.

When your view of the market is exclusively from the perspective of market research statistics, there is a big temptation — and in my view a dangerous one — to reject some potential customers.

When you look at a market research report, it's very easy to over-segment your market and say:

"We're not here to cater for that kind of customer."
Or:
"That kind of customer is not one of ours."
However, it's a totally different situation when you

are actually in face-to-face contact with customers, and one of them says:

"I won't be back."

Then, if you are truly customer-driven, it will hurt hard. I believe that the real entrepreneur is always spurred on by a wish to have every customer — by a childlike belief that you can win all the time, every time. Of course, you never achieve that — but the point is that you try.

For many years now, niche marketing has been highly fashionable. It is an approach that has obvious merits in some situations, but it can be taken too far. I believe that it is better to let the market define your niche, rather than to set your own limits on your ambitions.

I believe this for two reasons: first, the marketplace is constantly changing, far more than we realize. Second, and even more important, that what we know about the marketplace is always at best an approximation of the truth.

Let me give you an example of this. When I started in business, wine-drinking was a very rare thing in Ireland. Wine was not sold at all in supermarkets, but in wine merchants and a few high-class grocery stores. The wine-drinker was a clearly defined type: typically middle to upper-class, sophisticated, well off, and probably well-travelled.

At one stage we decided to try selling wine in Superquinn. Now if we had looked very closely at that niche, we would never have tried to sell wine in most of our shops. The profile of our customers, for the most part, simply did not match the profile of the

121

wine-drinking niche. If we had followed the textbooks, we would have sold wine only in those shops where our customers came close to the wine-drinking profile.

However, we approached it in a different way. We made the wine available in all our shops, and waited to see what would happen.

A completely new market profile for wine-drinking developed.

Part of this had to do with our making it available, providing for the first time an opportunity for people to browse among bottles of wine and buy without having to show a supercilious assistant how little they knew about wine.

Part of it had to do with our reaching out to the new public, offering them the information about wine that had not been put before them up to then.

But part of the trend was due to things that had nothing to do with us at all, but had created a latent demand for wine that was now being satisfied for the first time. These were things like a steadily rising standard of living, the growth of foreign holidays right through the different strata of society, even the influence of foreign films and television.

These background factors were actually laying the groundwork for change that would quickly take wine-drinking out of a narrow niche and into the mainstream.

But if we had targeted our marketing solely within the confines of the original niche, this broadening out would certainly never have happened so fast and might not have happened at all.

People — the real, flesh-and-blood people of the marketplace — are amazingly varied and highly unpredictable.

People are far less "typical" than we would sometimes like to think.

And they do not live in niches.

Obviously, every seller of a product or a service will have a core market that can often be defined fairly closely in terms of the socio-demographic factors — age, sex, social class, etc. — and the newer psychographic factors. Equally obviously, you need to make sure that you are appealing effectively to your core market.

I am not quarrelling with any of that. What I am quarrelling with is the widespread tendency to write off every customer who does not fall neatly within the core. That is not the way to be customer-driven, and it is not the best way to grow.

If you succeed in seeing your customers as people, I think you will be infected with the very human desire to serve them all.

I suggest that the way to do that is to make sure that your products are broad enough to appeal *both* to your core market, *and* to other potential customers from outside your existing core.

This need not mean being "all things to all men." That has its own dangers.

But it does mean that you should avoid focusing so narrowly that you run the risk of having the tide of market demand go out on you. If that happens, it may leave you high and dry in a narrow little cove from which there is no way to escape profitably.

123

The next time you are tempted to say, "Which will we go for, this market or that one?" try asking yourself: "Can we not go for both?"

In our business, we learned very early on that in almost everything you do there are options — options in terms of the people you set out to appeal to, options in the products you sell, options in the way you offer products.

And that there is a big danger in excluding options without very careful thought.

A simple example of this in retailing is the selling of multiple products — five apples for one dollar, five doughnuts for one dollar, that sort of thing. There are lots of variations: banding together two different but related products, for instance.

This is a standard kind of business-builder, and like all retailers we found it certainly was worthwhile. But it is important to remember that it does not suit everybody to buy products in multiples. And if it is the only option you offer, you will cause resentment among those who do not want to buy that way.

The temptation to exclude options sometimes occurs because we are infatuated — infatuated by a glamorous, exciting trend that has just appeared over the horizon. You must always remember that emerging trends get more than their fair share of attention.

An example is the trend towards healthy eating, one of the most important trends in food over the past 20 years.

Anyone who is in the business of producing or selling red meat ignores at their peril the fact that

there is now a solid core of 20 percent of people who
have decided to cut down or eliminate altogether
their consumption of red meat. In meat-eating
countries, this is a really major threat.

However, it should not blind us to the fact that, at
the same time, there is another 20 percent whose consumption of red meat is *increasing* — though they are
eating it in non-traditional forms like hamburgers.

What is even more interesting is the remaining
60 percent. These include those who move from one
category to the other — those who eat healthily some
of the time, and then at other times indulge in
different kinds of food.

So the danger of over-niching is that you can pass up
very sizeable business opportunities that exist outside
the narrow boundaries of the niche.

If you run a vegetarian restaurant, you are obviously
appealing to vegetarians. But if you offer *only*
vegetarian dishes, then you are making it much less
likely that your vegetarian customers will choose
your restaurant when they have friends with them
who are non-vegetarian.

Can you afford to turn away that market? That is the
question that should decide how you position
yourself. (I have a personal interest in this, because
my wife is a vegetarian and if we go to an exclusively
vegetarian restaurant I am forced to eat vegetarian
whether I feel like it that evening or not.)

Again, I am certainly not saying that you should
ever exclude options — merely that you should do so
reluctantly. In Superquinn we specialize in food; we
do not, for instance, sell textiles, or hardware, or toys

— as some of our competitors do.

Why have we closed those options off?

Our thinking was that we wanted to be best at whatever we did. I believe very strongly that long-term profitability is always founded on some competitive advantage which you first establish and then maintain.

We decided, when we had been in business long enough to get a feel for the marketplace, that we could be the best in our region in food. And we set that as a corporate objective, which gave a specific direction to our approach for over 20 years.

In deciding to be best in food, we didn't decide to exclude anything else. But whenever the opportunity to move into other areas arises, we ask ourselves two questions:

- Can we be best in this activity?
- Do we need this activity to keep our market broad enough?

If the answer to the first question is "no," then we are reluctant to go into the new activity. The reason is that we feel doing things we are not best at would compromise our overall reputation for quality, and therefore undermine our competitive advantage.

But even so, if the answer is "no," we still ask the second question. This guards against the danger of carving out too small a niche for ourselves.

In saying "no" to a market opportunity, we still want to appeal right across the board — to as many customers as we can. If we feel that to close off the opportunity would reduce the broad base of our appeal too much, then we look harder for ways to become best at the activity.

The guiding principle is: see your customers as people, and you will become reluctant to let any of them go.

Your basic instinct as a customer-driven person should be to embrace as many customers as possible, not to reject them. A customer-driven person's perspective should be positive, not negative.

You can develop that positive outlook by learning to see your customers as *people.* And the lesson of this chapter is that seeing your customers as people is what being customer-driven is all about.

CHAPTER 10

The secret weapon:
availability

AT THIS POINT, I HAVE an important job to do.
I want to correct an impression you may have got in
reading this far.

What we have been talking about all along is getting
the feel of the marketplace through personal, direct
contact with your customers. The impression that you
may have got is that you must always be the one to
initiate that contact.

This is not so.

When you are truly customer-driven, you will find
that much of your most valuable contact with
customers is initiated by *them* — not you.

And all you have to do is make it possible, let it
happen.

Contact that is initiated by customers rather than by
you is more valuable because they and not you are
setting the agenda.

I learned this lesson in my father's holiday camp,
Red Island.

Each evening during the four-month holiday season,
he took his meal in the main dining-room where the
500 guests were eating.

This didn't take him away from his family, because
we all ate there too. But it did mean that every one of
his meals was interrupted again and again by guests

who would see him there and come over to have a word.

My mother didn't particularly like these interruptions, but they were exactly what my father wanted. In fact, he positioned our table to encourage them. We were not hidden away in a corner, but placed near the entrance to the dining-room where nobody could fail to see him.

He was not just trying to show that he and his family ate the same food as the guests. It went beyond that.

He wanted to make it *easy* for guests to approach him.

Of course, he was around the holiday camp all the time during the day. And if people had a serious problem he was not difficult to find.

But what he was particularly anxious to elicit was the informal contact about things that were not "serious," but which could be important to the customer's satisfaction.

It worked. Again and again, people came up to him in the dining-room and talked to him about things they would never have sought him out in his office about. It was easy for them to do, and they knew he would be there every evening.

His *feel* for his customers was greatly enhanced by making himself available in this way.

Of course there was a *cost.*

He — and we — gave up some of his privacy. In his case, it was only for the four months of the summer season each year. But I am sure that if Red Island had been a year round business we would have been eating in the main dining-room every night of the year.

This is part of the price that the customer-driven person must pay to achieve the closeness to the customer that is vital. Believe me, it is a price worth paying

In Superquinn, we have always tried to ensure that we are highly available to customers. This applies to me, but not only to me — it applies right through the organization.

So we encourage our managers to do as much of their business as they can right out on the shop floor, where customers can see them — and where customers can approach them if they want to.

One of the ways we encourage this is by not giving them big, comfortable offices to hide themselves in.

A Superquinn manager's office is, quite deliberately, tiny and spartan — the bare minimum that is needed for the occasional meeting that must be held in private.

But a surprisingly large number of meetings do not need to be held in private. They can be held "in the marketplace."

I stumbled on this discovery as our company grew. I was always concerned that, as the business became more complicated, I would be drawn further and further away from the contact with customers that was the oxygen fuelling our success.

No matter how firm my resolution, I found myself spending less and less time on the floor of our shops. There were always pressing matters to be attended to in the office, especially meetings.

Then I discovered that many of the meetings I had did not have to be in my office. I began meeting people on the shop floor.

Yes, this sometimes means that meetings take longer. This is because, like our family dinners at Red Island, they are constantly interrupted by customers coming up to me to have a word. But it is not time lost.

For one thing, it gives the people I am meeting an insight into what customers are really like. Sometimes this can be directly relevant to their business, even to the subject of the meeting.

For instance, I remember meeting with Bill Lilley, the head of Coca-Cola in Ireland, in the part of our shop where the soft drinks are sold. Several times during the meeting we were approached by customers who had specific problems concerning Bill's product.

He went off saying that he had learned more about his marketplace during the short meeting with me than he had in the previous six months!

We hear a lot in management circles these days about *visible* leadership. The focus is usually on managers being visible to their staff, which I agree is vital. We hear **less** about the need to be visible to our customers, but it is equally vital — and that is what availability is all about.

So don't hide from your customers. Don't play hard to get. Make it easy for them to approach you. If you make yourself available, they will soon get to know about it.

Availability applies to more than just face-to-face communication. It applies also to letters and telephone calls.

I have a rule that letters from customers should, in the first instance, be answered by the person they were addressed to. It's not too difficult to do, but it's important.

Nobody likes to feel that their communication has been intercepted, particularly if they write to the top person and then get a reply from a "customer service department."

When that happens, it is the same as saying that the person they wrote to doesn't have the time to deal with customers.

When I was chairman of the Irish postal service, I got a lot of mail direct from the public about one aspect or another of the service. Almost always those letters had to be passed on to the people in the organization who could provide the proper response.

But I made sure to acknowledge each letter, telling the customer what I was doing.

In Superquinn, if a customer rings my office and asks to speak to me, I will take the call if I am there and free.

Why not? It does not really take up very much of my time, and the benefits are enormous.

Equally, I believe in being available to the media because that is an indirect way of being available to my customers.

Even when Superquinn was very small, with just a few shops, we always got more media coverage than much bigger firms in our business. I was always in the papers, being quoted on any issue that involved retailing.

This happened very simply. Because I tended to accept telephone calls from everybody, journalists quickly came to realize that I could be relied on for a quote.

It did us an immense amount of good in the marketplace, because our customers liked the feeling of dealing with people who were important enough to be quoted in the papers all the time. It also helped to get over to customers the idea that we were approachable and genuinely interested in our customers' problems.

It also, incidentally, gave me experience in understanding the needs of the media, particularly the time pressures they work under.

So simply being available is an important weapon in the struggle to become customer-driven. I call it a secret weapon because so few people know about it, so few people use it. Because that is so, it offers yet another opportunity to create a competitive advantage.

All right. Now let's look at this from a broader perspective, because being available is a part of a wider principle that is even more important.

The "center of gravity" of a business should be kept as close as possible to the point where the action is — where the business meets its customers.

Why?

Because it ensures that the energy of the organization is concentrated in the right place — towards generating customer satisfaction and so ensuring that they come back to do more business with you.

134

If you are customer-driven, the most important place in the company is not the boardroom but the marketplace. You can reflect this in the way you do business.

For instance, I have always believed in having a small head office organization. One of the things that diverts attention from serving the customer is the internecine strife that always seems to go on between head office and the units in the field.

So the smaller you keep your head office, the more you will contain that problem.

But recently I came to the conclusion that the problem was not so much the size of the head office, but the way it was seen. Most organizations are structured so that the head office is where the action is, and keeping head office happy becomes the name of the game.

How do you correct this perception, and get the energy focused on the customer?

Simple: abolish the head office!

This is what we have done in Superquinn. We no longer have a "head office."

What we do have is a "support office."

It's the same people, doing the same jobs, as in the old head office.

But now there's a clear signal to everyone as to how this part of the organization fits in with the rest: it's there to provide support to the people who deal directly with the customers.

At our new support office, we have a "swear-box." Everyone who utters the words "head office" has to put 25 cents into the box every time they offend!

135

But this is not a cosmetic change — it's a very fundamental one.

It involves a complete rethink by people about the company structure.

This is what I mean by shifting the center of gravity of the company to where the action is. The company should be sharply focused on the point where it meets customers.

For many years I have had a dislike of organization charts.

One of the reasons is because any hierarchical structure usually gives a very lowly rating to the customer interface.

A typical organization chart will be in the form of a pyramid:

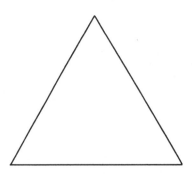

What this is saying is that the further up the pyramid you go, the more important things get.

But at what point of the pyramid does the company meet with its customers?

Very often it will be right down at the bottom.

This is certainly true of service organizations — like

banks, hotels, and supermarkets.

Most of their dealings with customers are made by people who the organization chart says are least important.

Any person who is truly customer-driven must feel very uneasy with a chart like this.

And again, we are not dealing with cosmetics here — these things determine how people think about an organization.

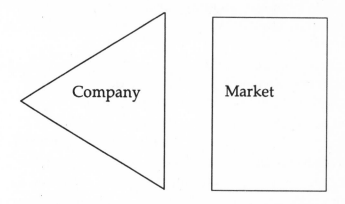

Look how easy it is to see things differently.

Turn the pyramid on its side, and add to it by including the marketplace.

Now we have a very different picture.

First of all, the chart includes the marketplace reminding everybody that the customers are an essential part of the company.

Second, it dramatizes the fact that the people closest to the marketplace are those who have direct contact with customers.

And third, it emphasizes the reverse of the second point — that the people at the "top" of the organization *are the farthest away from the marketplace.*

The "mental map" that a chart like this creates is very different to the one created by the conventional hierarchical one.

This is the kind of map that should be in the mind of a person who is truly customer-driven.

When you view your business world this way, the time you spend getting close to the customer suddenly seems to be much more relevant.

The idea of holding meetings and doing your business out in the marketplace seems on the ball, not off the wall.

And for everyone working in the organization, the critical importance of the people who deal with customers the most is properly emphasized.

If you are at the top of your organization, you can mastermind this shift in the center of gravity yourself. If you are not at the top, then you can still influence your organization by becoming an apostle for this kind of approach.

At the very least, you can make the shift just in your own mind — and by doing that alone, you will get very useful results.

I have found that when you genuinely see the key point of your organization as the place where the business meets the customers, it colors your view as to the things that have to be done centrally.

Let me give you **one example** of this.

Any company that exists in a fast-changing environment — and that is most companies, these days — needs to keep an eye on what is happening in its business right across the world.

All your new ideas don't have to be your own. Why reinvent the wheel if you can piggy-back on someone else's discovery?

So, as a matter of policy, our company subscribes to every English-language retailing trade magazine in the world. That way, in theory at least, we know about every new development almost as soon as it happens.

Now, you would say, sifting this mountain of information is obviously a "head office" task. Even a "support office" should do it, surely — as a service to its branches?

We found a different way, and one which I think is far more effective. We pick out a large number of young, fairly junior people spread across the company, and take out a subscription to one trade paper for each of them.

Then we say to them:

"You are the only person in the company — the only person in Ireland, in fact, — to be getting this particular trade paper each week. So you are our eyes and ears as to what's happening in New Zealand (or wherever).

"Your task is to read that paper every time you get it, scouring it for any development that you think might be of use to us here in this company."

Now what this means is that these papers are being read, not by some head office bureaucrat or some outside consultant, but by people who actually deal with our customers day in and day out.

It's a task that is actually done *better* the closer to the marketplace it happens — because the connections are more easily seen there.

Our experience is that the young people concerned relish this task, and sometimes it pays off in a big way.

In 1982, one young man in our Naas shop read about a grocer in California who had put a salad bar into his supermarket. Up to then, salad bars had only appeared in restaurants.

"Why not do it here in Naas?" he asked his manager.

"Let's have a go," said the manager and within four weeks they proved that it worked. It pleased customers and made a profit.

Within a further four weeks we had one in each of our shops, all doing well. It was six months later that we read in a trade magazine that a Brussels supermarket was going to open the Continent's first salad bar. We had been running them successfully for over half a year by then!

The lesson of this chapter is that customer-driven people are those who see that the most important place in their company is the point where the business meets the customers.

And who realize that that point is precisely where they should be, *available* to their customers.

CHAPTER 11

The jokers in the pack:
fun and surprise

BECOMING AND STAYING SUCCESSFUL in a
competitive marketplace is a very *serious* business.

Right?

Well, yes and no.

Yes, in the sense that very important issues are at
stake.

People's jobs, for instance. The difference between
having a secure future and being unemployed or
bankrupt is a very serious one.

Yes, too, in the sense that serving customers well
always needs to be approached in a highly
professional manner.

Your customers' needs are important to them: you
fail to take them seriously at your peril.

But being serious in this way does not mean that
there is no room for fun in the relationship with
customers.

On the contrary.

I believe there is a real need for fun.

Look at it this way. Suppose your customers have a
choice between two companies. Suppose that what
they offer is exactly alike in most ways. The quality is
the same, the price is the same, the delivery is the
same.

But suppose, too, that these companies differ in one

respect.

One is more enjoyable to deal with.

Which one will your customers pick?

In my experience, there is no contest. They will pick the company they enjoy dealing with.

Now let's not get carried away here.

I am not claiming that hard-nosed buyers, whether they are housewives or industrial buyers, make their purchasing decisions by asking themselves: "Who is more fun to deal with?"

In particular, I am not saying that an element of fun can substitute for competing effectively on quality and price.

What I am saying is that it can be the tie-breaker.

And the reason is that your customers are people, not impersonal organizations or machines.

Fun is a part of their lives, and they get very little of it in their business dealings.

I argued earlier that smiling is vital in building customer relationships. *Laughter is* equally important.

In my experience, people want to laugh. It is a great releaser of tension, and it is unequalled as a way of making people feel relaxed and at home in a strange environment.

Once again, I need to urge caution here. Humor can backfire, and you need to ease yourself carefully into it. But the element of fun can be introduced in other ways.

In retailing, of course, we are lucky. Our business lends itself to fun. All the same, I have no doubt that there are similar opportunities in all customer situations.

In Superquinn we celebrate at the drop of a hat. We try to celebrate everything.

Staff achievements.

Staff birthdays.

The birthdays of our shops.

And at the slightest excuse, we dress up. At Halloween, for instance, or when we are doing ethnic promotions. This introduces a carnival atmosphere right away.

Competitions, or giveaway promotions, are another sure-fire creator of fun in our business.

Sometimes in marketing, promotions are geared too much towards building extra business, there and then. But there should always be room for promotions that simply increase the customers' enjoyment.

Why?

Because increasing your customers' enjoyment is one way of ensuring that they come back to you.

These days all shops are full of special offers — they are a part of the marketing mix. We once took this to the ultimate extreme by putting price signs up on some goods like this:

We were giving the goods away, completely free. That wasn't a special offer — that was fun.

If you put yourself in the mood to create fun, you'll find opportunities in the most unlikely places.

For instance, one thing that always annoyed me was how often we misspelled signs by putting an apostrophe in the wrong place.

You know the sort of thing I mean: "Choice tomatoe's."

It was just a foible of mine, and no matter how many times I declared war on it we never seemed to get any better at preventing it.

So one day, when I was being interviewed for a New Year's radio program, I told the public that my New Year's resolution was to stop this once and for all. I asked them to help me by drawing our attention to every sign they found in our shops with a misplaced apostrophe.

Any customer who did this, I pledged, would get a free bottle of wine. (Of Piat D'Or, appropriately enough — a wine with an impeccable apostrophe of its own.)

I wasn't terribly serious about it, and certainly did not set out to create a major fun event. But that is exactly what happened.

The apostrophe hunt caught the public's imagination, and for months afterwards there were continuous press stories and letters to the editor about it.

In the shops, our customers entered into the spirit of it and scrutinized our signs as never before to find evidence of our mistakes.

They enjoyed themselves hugely. And we kept the

misplaced apostrophes at bay — for a while.

But if I had sat down to create a fun event, I doubt if in a million years I would have come up with that one. It just happened, because we were open to the idea of doing light-hearted things.

One manager told me that a customer had pointed out to him that we had six "illegal" apostrophes on our fish counter.

The assistant behind the counter had written:

"Fillet's of plaice, fillet's of sole, fillet's of mackerel," and so on.

"I only gave her one bottle of wine," he said. "Maybe I should have given her six."

I told the radio presenter, Mike Murphy, the story when he asked me how the campaign was going, and within a few minutes of it being mentioned on the radio, the customer was back in the shop to collect the five other bottles.

But that fish counter hasn't had a wrong apostrophe since!

We have found, too, that creating an enjoyable time for customers is not always a matter of us entertaining them. Sometimes customers create enjoyment by relating to each other.

An example of this is our "Romantic Evenings," the main object of which is to get our customers talking to each other.

It's all very light-hearted. When people come into the supermarket, they get a badge with a number on it. Men get a blue badge, women get a pink one. What they have to do is find their opposite number — the one other customer in the shop who has the same number as they do.

Any pairs who find each other can then claim a bottle of wine each as a prize.

The idea came from an American psychologist, who claimed that the best place to meet someone of the opposite sex was not in a disco or a night club but while doing your grocery shopping.

We decided to give it a try in our Blackrock shop, and I remember explaining on the John Bowman morning radio show that apparently you were less likely to feel rebuffed if your initial approach to a person who caught your fancy was, "Excuse me, have you tried this product before?"

Journalist Terry Keane, who was on the radio panel that morning, asked me: "But how would you know if the man was likely to be free?"

Thinking on my feet, I suggested to her that a box of baby's diapers in the shopping cart was an indication to try elsewhere, whereas half-bottles of wine, say, would show that a man was planning to eat on his own.

Terry immediately retorted: "I wouldn't regard someone who bought half-bottles of wine as a man — he would be a wimp!"

After that remark, broadcast to the nation, we noticed our sales of half-bottles dropped right away. But everyone agrees that our romantic evenings are great fun. The atmosphere in the shop when we hold one of them is something that has to be experienced. People relax and enjoy themselves, carrying out the unfamiliar task.

We have found that people are very ready to relax,

once they find that the situation allows it and encourages it.

Our customer namebadge weeks, which we do for the very serious purpose of getting to know our customers better, are in fact an occasion of fun for them.

And we have noticed over the years that as customers get used to the idea, they become more relaxed in the way they fill out their namebadge.

First time round, it's fairly formal.

Customers put "Mrs. McMahon" or "Mr. Kelly" on the badges.

The next time round, it becomes "Lorraine McMahon" or "Pat Kelly."

But then, when they get really used to the idea, it comes down to just first names.

Or even pet names.

The name badge week is a good illustration of the fact that you don't always have to put on a comedy show to create a sense of fun for the customers.

Anything that creates a feeling of shared experience among your customers will do the trick.

And if the word "fun" is still too strong for you, try starting off instead with the word "enjoyment."

This offers an excellent starting-point, because you can ask yourself the question:

"Is there any way in which dealing with us is *not* an enjoyable experience?"

If you focus on this, you will probably find "barriers to enjoyment" quite easily — barriers that you can do something about.

One of the biggest barriers we discovered was, as I

have described already, the problem of mothers shopping with young children.

That was a barrier to enjoyment of the shopping experience — not only for the mothers themselves, but also to a lesser extent for other customers in the shop.

Our playhouses were designed to remove that barrier to enjoyment.

When you have removed whatever barriers to enjoyment you discover, then you can move on to start creating the enjoyment.

And once again, don't be afraid that this has to mean getting out the jokebook — yet.

Consider the fact that all customers, no matter who they are and what the buying situation is, find it more pleasant to deal with a person who is in a good humor than with one who is not.

"Humor," in this sense, is highly infectious.

Talk to a person who is in a good humor, and some of it rubs off on to you.

Equally, bad humor rubs off just as effectively.

No wonder, therefore, that people prefer dealing with people who are habitually good-humored.

And why they often deliberately avoid people who are in a bad humor, when they have an opportunity to make a choice.

So there are three stages of making the customer's experience enjoyable:

- remove the barriers to enjoyment;
- make sure persons dealing with customers are always good-humored,

- create occasions of fun.

As important as fun in customer relationships, and closely linked to it, is the element of . . . surprise.

Any surprise won't do.

Remember that there are some things people don't want to be surprised about.

In our business, for instance, customers don't want to be surprised every time they walk into our supermarket by the fact that we have changed the position of the goods they want to buy.

Feeling familiar with the layout of the shop, and knowing where to look for any one of several thousand different products, is part of the enjoyment of shopping that they do not want disturbed.

However, within the familiar routine, they are delighted when they encounter something different.

It breaks the monotony of the routine, without destroying the value of the routine.

The very fact that most of our lives are full of routine creates the desire for change.

Consider the danger that your customers might go to a competitor rather than come back to you, *for no other reason than that they feel like a change.*

Far better, surely, then to provide them with a change yourself.

Surprise is closely related to fun because many of the things that create a sense of fun do so because they are unexpected, or a change from the routine.

At Club Med, for example, some evenings the ballroom becomes the dining-room and vice versa just to ensure that the thousand or so guests find their meal that night a break from the normal routine.

If a customer walks into one of our shops and finds all the checkout operators dressed up like St. Trinian's girls, it is the unexpectedness of it that creates much of the fun.

But there is a whole category of surprises that you can provide that has nothing to do with fun.

This is the surprise of "getting more than the deal."

At Red Island, my father used to greet guests on their arrival by offering them a cup of tea first.

"Come on in and have a cup of tea first, and then when you've had a chance to relax we'll check you in and show you to your room."

It suited him to do this, because otherwise large crowds of people would all be trying to check in at the same moment.

But people never failed to be charmed by the tiny gesture of generosity.

We do a similar thing each year the day before Mother's Day.

We hide a bucket of carnations under each checkout, and as women customers approach they are presented with a flower.

It's not "part of the deal." That's the whole point.

We do not advertise this in advance.

We do not shout out: "Come to Superquinn this weekend and get a free flower!"

This is something quite different from the practice of giving something free away with a purchase. "Buy a new car, and get a free vacation" — or whatever.

Incentives like that can be effective marketing tools, but they have nothing to do with what l am talking about here.

What I *am* talking about is encouraging customers to come back to you because you surprised them by giving something they did not expect — something that was not part of the deal between you.

We don't have a monopoly on this approach. Recently I took an early-morning flight from Dublin to London, one that leaves at 6 A.M. before any of the shops or other services at the airport are open.

When I got to the departure gate, I was surprised — and impressed — to see that Aer Lingus had prepared a serve-yourself coffee table, that the passengers could avail of before they boarded.

They didn't have to do it. Most people would not blame the airline for the fact that the airport services were not open at that hour. And the airline could very easily have said: "Sure we'll be giving them breakfast as soon as we take off."

But some customer-driven person realized just how important that little gesture could be, and how much the early-morning passengers would appreciate it.

They went the extra mile — and I have no doubt that the benefits far outweighed the tiny cost.

Fun and surprise: they are the jokers in the pack of the customer-driven person. Learn how to use them.

CHAPTER 12

Don't let the accountants win!

NOW LET ME FINISH BY TALKING very briefly about the bottom line.

Customer-driven people in companies always have to fight with people who have other priorities. For instance, many companies are totally cost driven.

They are so obsessed with always lowering costs that they find it very hard to look on any higher cost as an investment in future profit.

This isn't helped by the fact that sometimes the long-term benefit is hard to quantify. As I pointed out at the beginning of this book, this is where leadership comes in.

The leader must be prepared to back his instincts, and his instincts need to be right most of the time.

This is why it's important that the top person in the company is customer-driven. It's why I always heave a sigh of despair when I read that yet another accountant has reached the top job in an organization. It is not *impossible* for an accountant to become customer-driven, but it is an uphill task. All their training rebels against it.

Their focus is on the short-term and on the tangible and predictable.

The customer-driven focus tends to be on the long-term, and often has to live with factors that are intangible and less predictable.

But not *always*. And that is the point of this final word.

Neither the accountants nor you should fall into the trap of thinking that improving customer service always and inevitably means an increase in costs.

Sometimes you can have your cake *and* eat it.

Sometimes an improvement in customer service reduces costs at the same time.

As ammunition in your war against the accountants, let me give you **four** examples of this in action.

The first time I saw it happen was at my father's Red Island Holiday Camp.

Every week we had 500 guests and each morning they all had breakfast. They had a choice of porridge or cornflakes. About four out of five of them chose cornflakes.

My father's own preference was for porridge, but he always took it with cream rather than milk — in fact, he didn't like porridge with milk. And one day, looking at the breakfast operation, he said to himself:

"If I like it with cream, maybe other people would prefer it that way as well."

So he decided to serve the porridge with a little jug of cream rather than milk. He looked into the cost of it, and while of course the cream cost more than the milk, even the porridge with cream cost less than the cornflakes with milk.

So while changing to cream would cost him something, it was not a great deal. He decided to bear the extra expense and give the porridge-lovers a higher quality breakfast.

The porridge-eaters loved it. But they were not the

only ones. When the cornflake-eaters saw that you got cream with the porridge, many of them decided to switch to porridge as well.

In the end, my father had 400 people eating porridge and 100 eating cornflakes, instead of the other way round.

And therefore, though he hadn't set out to do that, he had also reduced his costs. For every person who switched from cornflakes with milk to porridge with cream, he saved some money.

And everybody was happy.

Years later, I saw the same win/win situation in California. The first time I went to San Francisco, I crossed a toll bridge to visit some supermarkets in Oakland.

As we went over the bridge, we had to slow down and line up to pay our 50 cents toll. A few hours later, we did the same on the way back. Not bad value for 50 cents.

A few years later I visited San Francisco again, and made the same trip across the toll bridge to visit those supermarkets. This time, to my surprise, we didn't have to slow down and we didn't have to wait in line. There was no toll, and we just whizzed through.

I remember being surprised at this, because it was a time of high inflation and very few prices were going down, anywhere in the world. As well as that, I knew that some American cities were in dire straits trying to make ends meet. So I was impressed that San Francisco had been able to do away with the toll on the bridge.

It was only when we came back a few hours later

that I discovered there still was a toll on the bridge but in one direction only, and that the toll fee had been doubled to a dollar.

What they had done was this: They discovered that practically everyone made pairs of trips across the bridge. You went across the bridge, you had to take it back. Therefore if they caught everybody once instead of twice, but doubled the toll, they would end up with the same income.

But not, of course, the same costs. Because they had entirely removed one half of the toll-collecting operation. While at the same time improving the quality of service to their customers, since drivers now did not have to delay at all on the outward crossing.

Win/win. Improved customer service and lower costs, at the same time.

I am pleased to say that I have experienced some of these delightful situations in my own business, and I am convinced that if you are customer-driven they will come to you — as a kind of blessing from the gods.

One example of it was when we had a request from customers to put in check weighing-scales for customers in the produce department.

Our system then was that customers selected their produce, put it into bags and brought it to an assistant to be weighed and priced. The problem some customers had was that they didn't know until the bag was weighed how much they had, and sometimes it was more than they wanted.

So with the check weighing-scales they could see

how much they had put into the bag before going up to the assistant. If they found that they had taken more than they wanted, they could just leave some back on the display.

We provided the weighing-scales in response to these requests. The scales had to tell them how much the produce they were weighing cost, so we had to use an electronic scales where they could press a button carrying the name of the product, and the scales would work out the price and display it.

Customers liked the system, and we got much praise for it. It was expensive, but I believed it was worth it.

However, the approach soon paid for itself handsomely. Because we realized that we could use scales that would print out the price on a sticker, which the customers themselves could attach to the bag and then take straight to the checkout.

This released staff, who had been weighing and pricing the customers' goods, to do more productive things.

Win/win. The customers had more control over what they bought, and were spared the hassle of waiting in line to have their produce weighed. We had improved our quality of service, and at the same time reduced our costs.

A final, more recent, example.

We have always packed our customers goods in plastic bags. In fact, this at one stage was a competitive advantage, because one of our competitors didn't give free bags at all — you had to pay if you wanted a bag.

However, nowadays everyone gives plastic bags

and we all accept it as a major but necessary expense doing business.

Last year, however, two of our staff at our Bray branch, Alison Crinion and Catherine Meany, were approached by a customer who said:

"I hate those plastic bags, because when I get home I have to keep making trips to the car to bring them inside a few at a time. Would you have a box that I could put all this stuff in, please?"

They got her a box, of course, and made a resolution to see that she was offered a box each time she was in. But then they got to thinking.

"Maybe other people would prefer boxes, too?"

Out of that came the idea that they would keep a stock of boxes by the checkout for use by any customers who preferred that way of packing.

They set that up. It wasn't difficult, we had boxes coming out of our ears. Each week at that shop we filled three skips full of discarded boxes for the compactor.

When they put the scheme into operation, they found they were right. Quite a few people saw the boxes and preferred that way of packing.

Seeing how much the customers appreciated it, they went one step further. They got into the habit of asking each customer whether they would prefer a box or the plastic bags.

And they found that even more customers said they preferred the boxes.

Lots of happy customers. It was a definite improvement in customer service.

When the arrangement was up and running, we

heard all kinds of reasons from customers as to why the boxes were better. Bread, for instance, didn't get crushed in a box whereas it did so much more easily in a bag.

But the best part was still to come. When the next quarter's figures came in, we discovered that there was a dramatic drop in the cost of plastic bags used at that shop. Not only that, but the cost of compacting the discarded boxes had also fallen: now we filled only one bin a week, instead of three.

Win/win. Better customer service, lower costs — at the same time.

The point here is that improved customer service need not *necessarily* cost you more money.

If it does, then you have to find a way of justifying it — usually over the longer-term.

But the fact that it often does cost more should not blind you to the fact that sometimes it can cost *less* to serve the customer better.

And everybody wins. Even those bloody accountants.